Gentle
Architecture

Gentle Architecture

Malcolm Wells

McGraw-Hill Book Company

New York St. Louis San Francisco Auckland
Bogotá Hamburg Johannesburg London Madrid
Montreal New Delhi Panama Paris São Paulo
Singapore Sydney Tokyo Toronto

Library of Congress Cataloging in Publication Data

Wells, Malcolm.
   Gentle architecture.

   Bibliography: p.
   Includes index.
   1. Architecture—Environmental aspects.   I. Title
NA2542.35.W44   720   80-19562
ISBN 0-07-069245-9

1234567890   VHVH   8987654321

The editors for this book were Jeremy Robinson, Joan Zseleczky,
and Susan Thomas; the designer was Naomi Auerbach; and the
production supervisor was Thomas G. Kowalczyk. It was set in Souvenir Light
by The Clarinda Company.

Printed and bound by Von Hoffman Press, Inc.

I wish I could dedicate something a little more like Walden *or* Leaves of Grass *to my wife, Sis, for the patience and help she's given me, but all I can offer her is this little book on construction and design.*
She and Dave Deppen did more than any others to launch me into a gentler architecture, and for that I'm very grateful.

Contents

Preface

You don't have to be very wise or very perceptive to see what a mess we've made of our beautiful earth. We're even paving large portions of our *national parks!*

To our grandparents, "the good old days" were those of a society just beginning to emerge from its pastoral phase, society delighted with *every* new invention. To us, "the good old days" sounds prenuclear, uncomplicated, low key, and generally rather wholesome. Whether we and our grandparents deceive ourselves about all that is, of course, open to question, but it is a fact that in those times that are gone forever, hazardous substances were less virulent, terrorism was unknown, and human society was thought to have continuing prospects for improvement.

Now think about what "the good old days" will mean to our children: just what they see around them today. It will be against this norm that they will measure the even greater horrors to come—unless we can start to turn in some new direction right now, unless the embryonic, and still largely misguided, environmental movement starts to produce the sweeping changes that must be made if we are to have any hope of survival.

I leave for other minds the solutions to such problems as the nuclear ones, geotoxification, desertification, and overpopulation. But I do have the temerity to offer some thoughts on the ways in which the *built* world has got to be changed. It is, after all, more visible, more manageable, than radiation; its effects are more easily measured than those of desert growth. We can tell from our man-made environment, sometimes at a single glance, whether we're getting deeper into or climbing out of trouble. For this we don't have to wait two or three generations, as we must to see if we've caused genetic damage or if we've melted the polar ice. Architecture of every kind, as slowly as it sometimes seems to evolve, is faster than all that. And we can get started on the new kind right away.

Malcolm Wells

The Mole found himself placed next to Mr. Badger, and, as the other two were still deep in river gossip from which nothing could divert them, he took the opportunity to tell Badger how comfortable and homelike it all felt to him. "Once well underground," he said, "you know exactly where you are. Nothing can happen to you and nothing can get at you. You're entirely your own master, and you don't have to consult anybody or mind what they say. Things go on all the same overhead, and you let 'em, and don't bother about 'em. When you want to, up you go, and there the things are, waiting for you."

The Badger simply beamed on him. "That's exactly what I say," he replied. "There's no security, or peace or tranquility, except underground. And then, if your ideas get larger and you want to expand—why, a dig and a scrape, and there you are! If you feel your house is a bit too big, you stop up a hole or two and there you are again! No builders, no tradesmen, no remarks passed on to you by fellows looking over your wall, and, above all, no weather. Look at Rat now. A couple of feet of floodwater, and he's got to move into hired lodgings; uncomfortable, inconveniently situated, and horribly expensive. Take Toad. I say nothing against Toad Hall; quite the best house in these parts, as a house. But supposing a fire breaks out—where's Toad? Supposing tiles are blown off, or walls sink and crack, or windows get broken—where's Toad? No, up and out of doors is good enough to roam about in and get one's living in; but underground to come back to at last—that's my idea of a home!"

KENNETH GRAHAME
The Wind in The Willows

Living Room

When I was a little kid my big brother taught me how to draw by forcing me to look at familiar things in unfamiliar ways. For instance, he made me read words upside down, or identify things with my eyes closed. I never knew *what* he was going to put into my hand! Sometimes, he described in nauseating detail the tumbling landscape I'd see if I were strapped to the side of a Ferris wheel. And he showed me how our house might look, as seen from an airplane. Once, he asked me to make the marching sounds a germ might hear if a caterpillar walked by. Another time, he had me paint a landscape in the complements of its true colors: orange sky, red grass, purple sun.

But the exercise I always liked best was that of lying on the living room floor, trying to imagine it as a ceiling to which I was fastened, the actual ceiling having become the floor. For the first few moments, the new "floor" refused to be anything but the old familiar ceiling, upside down, but then something in my mind would shift, and the ceiling would no longer be a ceiling. It would become a floor, the strange new floor of a room above which our furniture dangled precariously while our dog walked, fly-fashion, across the overhead rug. At each doorway, a foot-high threshold promised to trip anyone foolish enough to make a careless entrance, and a wallpapered ramp sloped down, below the inverted stair, to the bedrooms "below."

I can't begin to tell you how many boring lectures I've survived by roaming the inverted ceilings of the auditoriums in which they were given. My brother helped make the world more exciting for me. As a result, even though I hardly consider myself an artist, I can at least produce a simple perspective drawing—and I enjoy reading any upside down words I happen to see.

Fun on the living room floor and fading memories of Depression-era art lessons must seem like strange matters with which to introduce a serious book on deadly subjects, but this book is built on two ideas: *living room* (in many senses of the word) and new perspectives. These are two ideas that come to mind whenever I remember the things my brother tried so hard to teach me.

How seldom we use our imaginations! That splendid capacity for mental adventure lies buried in each of us under all the layers of conformity that school and television and a paperwork avalanche have created. Not unless we get high do we even dare let ourselves respond to the stimuli, to all the wild impulses, that wash over us all the time. We turn them off, and lose much of our capacity for wonder.

My brother made me wonder about all sorts of things. He gave me a picture of heaven I still prefer to most others: a heaven on earth in which I can look behind the scenes of all the events that ever happened; see instant replays of everything, endlessly satisfying an endless curiosity. Sometimes I think I'd start, if the choice were mine, by choosing simple revelations, like arranging, when I'm in a crowd, to have a tiny red light glow for a moment above the head of every uncaught criminal there, or of everyone who'd made love in, say, the last half hour. I'd be fascinated by the findings no matter what they showed.

Or maybe I'd choose to see lighted paths appear everywhere I'd walked during my lifetime. ("I don't ever remember being *there!*") Next, I might switch to wider subjects, choosing to see, in living color, the entire life of Abraham Lincoln, innermost thoughts and all. Or, if any such places were left on earth, to see where no human foot, in all of history, had ever trod. And sooner or later, of course, I'd get around to Henry. I'd want to know all about that man.

Henry Thoreau died more than a hundred years ago, but, as is true of so many other Thoreau fans, I have him with me often. I look through his quiet gray eyes in order to see more clearly the world in front of mine. Witnessing his first view of the modern world was one of the saddest moments of my life. He couldn't believe what we'd done to the pastoral countryside he'd known, or understand how we could bear to leave it this way.

Watching his first takeoff as a jet passenger or seeing him view today's

Boston for the first time was enough to make me momentarily wise, his first driving lesson enough to make me momentarily hysterical. "No, Henry, *no!* Your *right* foot. Your *right* foot!"

It's hard for us to see this world without such help. We're too damned adaptable, that's the trouble. Who can still remember what stood on the corner before the burger joint was built? We live in the all-too-familiar *now,* which never seems to change, unmoved by any event more that 48 hours in the past. We have no anchors in our drift through time.

Seeing the world from other points of view—historical, physical, biological, social, geological—sometimes helps us see the present moment, and ourselves, in perspective.

This is an architectural point of view.

CHAPTER ONE

Commitment

We all know that buildings destroy land, and yet in the name of architecture we continue to pave this beautiful country with buildings and parking lots. Every one of us in the building industry or paving industry does his part. Where there were forests there is now concrete. Where there were prairies we find asphalt. Where there were meadows, houses have appeared. Architects, along with engineers, builders, pavers, realtors, developers, mortgagors, planners, and building officials, have created so much momentum in so many wrong directions we can't seem to stop, even though many of us now know we're in trouble. Listen to what the members of a New York AIA jury, architects themselves, had to say: "Architects have not yet struck out on any firm new directions away from the modern movement."[1] And in California, it was a *citizens'* group that had to petition the California Board of Architectural Examiners before it would even consider requiring architects to take courses in such subjects as insulation, solar heating and cooling, and appliance efficiency.[2] As a profession, we're still arguing about building styles at a time when the very foundations of modern architecture are in question.

We're really out of touch.

Most of us respond directly, intuitively, to natural beauty or to the beauty of the best indigenous architecture. We sense its appropriateness. It feels right. Most modern architecture, on the other hand, now feels wrong. (It *literally* feels wrong when the fuels run out.) Look-alike buildings in look-alike cities were the architecture of abundance. Now the abundant age is past, and the validity of all the things we took to be architectural certainties is called into question.

The best-known architects of the day create stunning forms and impressive details, but there is little substance behind them. It's not that the architects don't know better. They do. We all do, by now. Modern architecture is empty because we still lack the courage to face its consequences.

[1] *The New York Times,* Mar. 13, 1977.
[2] *Not Man Apart,* Mid-March, 1977.

I pushed a button, a few minutes ago, to light eight rows of fluorescent fixtures in a huge office space, simply to see if I'd left an old tweed jacket there. I didn't even think about what would happen in addition to all that lighting when I touched the switch, my judgment was so well deactivated by a half century of power company advertising. I didn't think about the all-too-familiar consequences of wasted electricity. It's too bad I didn't have to go through a ten-minute countdown in order to energize that circuit. Then I might have thought before I acted.

When I pushed that lighting button (instead of simply waiting for a moment, letting my eyes adjust to the darkness, and then looking for the jacket at the desk and chair I'd been using), I caused another bit of this American land to be stripped in the search for coal, or another bit of lethal radiation to swell the containment vessel of a nuclear power plant, or another cupful of oil to be precariously conveyed in some tanker. I knew better but I didn't want to think about all the consequences. Obviously, I had not yet made a solid commitment to saving electricity.

There are, of course, those who would say that my button pushing was actually patriotic, generating, as it did, not only the need for more electricity but wealth and jobs as well; but the hollowness of such arguments is increasingly apparent. We know where such reasoning has led us in the past.

Life without the courage to face consequences is cowardice, and life teems with it today. Look at the headlines. The incredible cowardice shown by a terrorist in the taking of children as hostages is monstrously embarrassing, yet the cowardice of his act gets overlooked in most accounts of the event. He arrives home to a hero's welcome.

Who would have imagined a time would come when cowards were called heroes!

Cowardice in the practice of architecture and the cowardice of the terrorist are worlds apart, but their effects can be equally long-lasting; a building can destroy land and waste resources for a hundred years or more.

Values

How far down this list should the paving over of *100 acres of prime farmland* be pegged?

1. Terrorism
2. Hostage-taking
3. Skyjacking
4. Kidnapping

5. Assault with a deadly weapon
6. Rape
7. Vandalism
8. Graffiti
9. Litter
10. Obscene phone calls

Should such farm destruction follow number 3? Number 4? Number 5? Or should the mere paving of land not *even* appear on a list like this? It's hard to attempt value judgments when human lives and property are weighed against land values, isn't it? And yet the question has got to be faced. We must put values on all things if we are to act responsibly.

How much am *I* worth? Is my life equal to one square foot of mature forest land? Two feet? An acre? A square mile? How about a hundred acres or a whole state—how many human lives are *they* worth? Before rejecting such speculation as irrelevant nonsense, remember the kinds of things we go to war for.

In the Great Library of Heaven there are said to be ancient books in which the values of all things are written, but we can't get inside the gates, let alone see the books. We must work such things out for ourselves. There seems to be some urgency about the matter, too, if a lot of very impressive people are to be believed. It's awfully late in the day for us architects to be still dragging our feet on the question of life values. Obviously, you wouldn't want to weigh, *for someone else's conscience,* the exact value of an arm or a leg, a tree or a pond. But responsible living must be based on some rational system of values.

Maybe, of course, just getting the matter aired is enough; maybe if we do nothing more than acknowledge the existence of values other than those shown on the bodily-injury and property-damage tables of insurance companies we'll have made a start. I don't know. I *do* know that we're wrecking this country with our failure to face the consequences of our acts.

Don't misunderstand. We ask surgeons to do things we'd be too squeamish to do, but, all squeamishness aside, few of us have any *moral* objections to surgery. Squeamishness is not cowardice. It's a different story, however, when it comes to hamburgers. We'd not only be squeamish about watching the slaughter of a healthy steer: most of us, face-to-face with its moment of execution, might balk and go for peanut butter instead, on some sort of *moral* ground. In the slaughterhouse the *consequences* of a hamburger tend to outweight its appeal. And yet, out of sight, out of mind: we reestablish our special kind of cowardice with the next bite of a Giant Double Whoppie.

This is not a plea for vegetarianism (although there are impressive health and world-food-supply statistics to support the case for that way of life). The pointy little pairs of fangs we brush each night, those teeth located three places off center, probably didn't grow in our mouths for nothing. Still, how many of us have decided the matter down at the staughterhouse, in the presence of the cattle? How may of us have even faced the question?

This pretending there are no consequences rages through modern society. We are encouraged from all sides not to look beyond immediate gratification. And nowhere, it seems, is this attitude more common or more heavily cloaked in hypocrisy than it is in architecture. As a group we architects simply will not face the consequences of our own plans and specifications. It isn't that our hearts aren't in the right places; we all want the best for America. But we sometimes forget that each line we draw can actually destroy life. Whether that line represents a site contour due for reshaping by a bulldozer, or a two-by-four to be torn from a forest, life of some kind is always at stake.

Architecture has a moral side which must be faced. If we ever find a way to build with proper respect for this planet our reward can be more than just environmental. It can be aesthetic, too, perhaps beyond our wildest dreams. But first we've got to commit ourselves, *for life,* to the idea of land-respect. Without such commitment our efforts will be useless.

The environmental movement, which first captured wide attention in the late sixties, is now represented by scores of college-level programs, hundreds of save-the-land organizations, vast government bureaucracies, thousands of books, and millions of concerned citizens, and yet our environment is getting worse all the time.

I see fire in the eyes of lecture audiences, and I hear moving words from highly placed people, but little happens. It's almost as if an ecological concern were regarded, even by its supporters, as a second-class cause, something having not quite the same stature, say, as the abortion issue or Middle East politics. In matters of ecology, the environment, conservation, we're still mushy and spineless, and the old ways die hard. Worst of all, perhaps, is the smugness that we who do a bit of good, environmentally, show to those who do not, when in reality we are both living far too high on the hog. In a starving world, with millions of Americans out of work, and with skies so smoky they present a serious collision hazard to aircraft, with land eroding and water supplies growing toxic, we congratulate ourselves and talk of new priorities, forgetting that the whole, tottering structure of precedent, law, tradition, and officialdom, which holds our society together, is but the frothiest of icings, bound to melt away the minute the food runs out and the wells run dry. Then it will be right back to tooth and claw again. That's probably the only way we'll ever really change. But what a shame! We could forestall such a disaster. We could all be better housed, all be living in beautiful, green cities under sparkling skies, if we made some commitments in advance of disaster—commitments in the nature of: "This is as far as I will go." Then we wouldn't be caught sitting on the fence when the real test came. We should decide right now not to participate in obviously harmful practices, not to cooperate, for instance, with anyone who talks about unlimited industrial growth, nuclear power, or pollution controls.*

Changing the vast machinery of industry and government isn't a hopeless task involving billions of hours, endless political campaigns, or even violent revolution. It can all start the minute something, up behind the eyes somewhere, goes "click."

Electric Heating

Electric resistance heating is one of the most wasteful of all kinds of energy use. A lot of people's electric heating bills are showing that it's a good way to waste money as well. The more you learn about electric heat, the more appalling it seems that it is even allowed. It is the worst choice—and not just for heating entire buildings. Almost every time you heat something electrically, you become part of an energy-wasting process that borders on the criminal.† Now that I know this I am *commited* to the idea of not using electricity for any heating task another energy form can handle. (So far, however, I've made no strong commitment on the toast question.) Now I no longer have to wonder where I stand when the matter comes up. Having read of Three Mile Island and black lung, I don't want to waste electricity, period. Wasteful electrical use moves us closer and closer to total dependence upon nuclear power and the mining of America.

When I built my first underground building, I made several mistakes, but the biggest one was that of using electric heat. I thought it was as clean and efficient as the power company had said it was. That was in 1970. Now I know better. Now I know that energy has not only quantity but quality. To use a very precious and sophisticated form of energy like electricity for a very unsophisticated purpose like heating is a perversion of all conservation principles, and of architecture as well.

Properly designed heat pumps are another story. With them, you can

---

*Pollution controls simply make official dumping grounds of all our skies and waters. Waste management, *before* pollution occurs, is the only sensible course.

†Even hydro-power-generated electricity is too good, too sophisticated, to use for heating. Any fuel can provide warmth. Electrical power is for far more sophisticated uses.

often get three of four units of heat for *every* unit of energy put into the heating system. In such cases it may very well pay to go electric, but *don't guess,* and don't take the power company's word for it! Do some snooping around. Go to the local library, the community college, the bookstore, and the local solar or alternative energy organization. You'll find the names of people in your area who know what they're talking about. When you do, spend the money it takes to get their advice. There are few better investments. Today, a small cadre of solar designers and energy-conscious architects knows far more about energy, natural resources, equipment efficiency, and electrical alternatives than do many experienced mechanical and electrical engineers who were educated and who practiced years before any of us began to think about these things. That's why we're in trouble. We drift along in a world designed by generations of wasters, many of whom still refuse to face the consequences of their acts.

Dehumanization

Consequences are tied to every move we make. Listen to what Robert Finch has to say on the subject:

> Does hunting brutalize men? The hunters I have known personally don't suggest that it does. But, more than that, the principle behind such a question strikes me as false. From what I have seen, it is not proximity, but distance from death and destruction that brutalizes us. Such technological and economic distances that allow a bomber pilot to destroy a peasant village at 30,000 feet, or a real estate developer to wipe out a tract of woodland or marsh from an office in Boston, abstraction is what dehumanizes us. The hunter, at least, knows what it is he destroys.

Somewhere, right now, an architect is working at his drawing board. Each line he draws represents a physical change that will—if the bids are within the budget—take place somewhere, perhaps thousands of miles from where he sits. He destroys faraway places simply by drawing lines on paper. Down come trees, away goes topsoil, unnoticed. This is death by abstraction, too.

Sex

But if abstraction is what dehumanizes us, what is it that humanizes us? I'm tempted to say sex, even though the current view of sex in America is more one of pornography and violence than of regeneration and com-

---

[3]Robert Finch, "Soundings," *The Cape Codder,* June 13, 1978, p. 28. Used by permission.

mitment. Nature created the sex urge to keep the race alive. That's obvious. What isn't obvious is why that tender ache remains with us so long after the years of reproduction have passed. After all, it wasn't many generations ago when to be old was to reach 35, when a man of 50 was a patriarch. That was the human timetable, and human reporduction ages were surely scheduled to accommodate it. So what is this lust we feel at 40 and 50, and, from what I'm told, at 70? How can we, descended from and imprinted by those ancestors, have such long-lived sex interests? What's the point of them? All natural phenomena have a purpose. Nature isn't likely to let us waste all that creative energy for nothing. Is there a message in this middle-aged hunger, one that people of all ages might be well advised to heed? Can it be that among our distant ancestors those without these lingering lusts were bred out of existence, and out of our genes, by a natural selection which found such disinterest a fatal weakness in the race? Was it perhaps that to grow old without such feelings meant losing touch with the rhythms of life, losing a needed tolerance for the coupling passions of the young? Maybe those who lost their sex interest too soon lost their grasp of land husbandry and of the purposes of flowers and seed and harvest, and failed to produce enough food to last through the long winters. It's anyone's guess, of course, but *something* must have happened to give us these three-quarter-century distractions.

Here we are, a nation of increasingly older people, still responding to the point of foolishness whenever the right stimuli appear. The relevant questions with regard to all this are probably, "So, what? What's wrong with it?" But, considering how few other interests are as long-lived or as reliable, what can it teach us about living? And, with regard to architecture, what can we learn from our lusts about this next world we must build? There is, after all, a notable absence of lustiness, of earthy life-relatedness in our buildings. One has only to look at what passes for architecture downtown, or out along the strip, or in Ivy Green Ranchwood Acres, to see how phony, how empty and shallow, it all is. The only vestige of sex left in the act of construction seems to be in the language of steelworkers and steamfitters, and the only sex among completed buildings is in the sorry garishness of the store selling dirty books. But what if we saw *the building itself* as a potential sex object, not as a pile of bricks to fondle, but as a giver of life? What would happen if roofs and wall slopes become places for things to grow instead of places for cracked asphalt and graffiti? What if architects routinely brought dying land back to good health? We'd be bound to get healthier because of it. Anything would be better for us than what we're building now. Have you walked through Newark lately, or taken the train to Philadelphia? Have you seen the back side of Dallas or the alleys of Los Angles? Does the hopelessness, the cruelty, of what we've done to this country make despair tighten your throat? Is it at all related to the skin shows and sex shops that are sometimes the only signs of life left on the street? Is lust after forty a recent phenomenon, an industrial-age aberration we've manufactured to fill the vacuum left by our flight from the farms? Maybe this itch is simply a defense against emptiness, against our having been cheated out of the natural sex life of living things reproducing in a natural world. Regardless of that, or possibly because of it, architecture seems to be headed straight down the wrong track. The tragic perversion of our built world is now so obvious that even the most ardent boomers of technocracy can see it. I don't know of anyone who is truly satisfied with the direction in which we are heading.

You don't hear it said too much anymore, but architects used to enjoy quoting an 1800-year-old line by the Roman Vitruvius that went something like this, "The three basic qualities of architecture are commodity, firmness, and delight."

I've got to confess that when the proper occasions presented themselves, I could be heard to say those lines myself, in spite of my never having quite understood exactly what they meant. The nice thing was that, depending on how loosely you interpreted them, they could be stretched to fit almost any building.

Architectural Criteria

There are, however, more appropriate and less elastic criteria, the first of which is, obviously, safety—human safety. Without that, architects are out of business. Shelter without the quality of human safety is meaningless. Only after *it* has been assured are we able to think of the other creatures, of all the nonvoters that must share this ride, and it is for them, the plants and animals of the world, that we are beginning to evolve wider and more humane codes, and discovering, in the process, that such codes, if used in time, may also assure our own survival.

The problem is that we usually do no more than the building codes require of us, and so continue to foul our nest. Perhaps we can still escape blame for this on the grounds that our system of values was handed to us long ago, at home and at school, fully formulated, almost in the nature of commandments. Then and now, in all too many architectural schools, building-design criteria concentrate on form, dabble in sociology, and skim through function (which may or may not touch upon what it is that buildings actually do to the world we build them in). Energy costs, resource depletion and, above all, the life science itself, biology, are seldom taught.

It seems almost unthinkable that structures to house living beings in a living world could be conceived and executed in utter disregard of life values, but that's the way it is, and the building regulation bureaucracy, which fought modern architecture for so many years, now institutionalizes it. Environmental issues take second place, and sometimes no place at all, before the burning issues of parking-lot size and the proper filling out of forms. And those environmental impact statements! Many are outright lies.

Every day, I get stacks of mail from people who want detailed how-to-do-it building information. (What will happen with this case, how will this work, what do I do here?) I try to answer them, but I find, more and more, that many answers are descriptions of natural phenomena which never change. If we'd been taught such things from birth we wouldn't have to write letters to faraway architects asking what water will do under this circumstance, or what heat will do under that. Almost every successful architectural detail is based on nothing more abstruse than the fact that water can be counted on to freeze at 32° F, to run downhill, and to soak into porous materials. All the phenomena, in other words, that we see around us every day, are based, and will continue to be based, forever and ever, on fixed laws, most of which are quite easy to grasp. And yet, because those laws are involved with architecture, they suddenly become mysterious and profound, and we think that only an expert can deal with them.

Construction Fasteners

In 1966, I took my first timid steps toward a less destructive kind of architecture. I thought I was being daring, pushing back the frontiers of my profession, when I designed that industrial building at Reading, Pennsylvania. It was a long time before I realized that only because I had a kind and tolerant client was I able to try a few of the things I was starting to think about. Irvin Cohen had asked me to design a building to house all the company's activities, everything from manufacturing to administration. His products: bolts and screws. The company: Construction Fasteners Inc. The site: a few acres of badly overfarmed, eroded land on a barren hilltop outside the city. My solution: 20,000 square feet of space housed in a complex of sloping, shed-form buildings made of concrete and weathering steel, the roofs and parking lots of which drained their runoff into a percolation bed instead of into the storm sewers. Instead of

grass, crown vetch was the ground cover, and the entire site was planted with young trees. Now, 15 years and four additions later, the building has more than doubled in size but the site shows no trace of the misuse it had undergone before its purchase. In sharp contrast to the unrelenting asphalt of a giant shopping center just across the road, gardens and trees

FIG. 1.1 (upper) *Construction Fasteners' original building at Wyomissing, Pa., 1966. (Artog)*

FIG. 1.2 (lower) *Original proposal for the shed-cluster design of Construction Fasteners, 1966.*

cover every unbuilt foot of the Construction Fasteners site, wildlife abounds, and the runoff from the entire complex is still handled right there on the property. Each addition to the building gets better, environmentally. In the first, there were task lighting and extra insulation. Then came the use of exterior insulation and daylighting. Now passive solar heating has been added to the complex.

Over the years, the deep cover of nitrogen-fixing crown vetch has turned the original raw subsoil into healthier land. The vetch has also controlled erosion and helped slow the runoff of rain. It has offered the emerging trees no competition and has provided cover for all the small game that's flocked to the site. The giant percolation bed, looking more like a sculpture garden than a rain sink, continues to channel water into the ground instead of into the storm sewers. Things seem to get better every year at the Construction Fasteners site.

My original proposal, however, was for an underground building. I had just begun to advocate building in that way when the Construction Fasteners project came along. But by the same luck that kept all my other early underground designs from getting built, I was spared the embarrassment of seeing this one executed. All my early designs were so full of potential problems I often send a prayer of gratitude off in the direction of the gods for watching over me so well. Because of their vigilance, I was able to confine most of my underground mistakes to my own office building; and I was even able to correct some of them before I sold it. My underground design for Construction Fasteners would have generated all sorts of troubles. For one thing, it would have made it virtually impossible

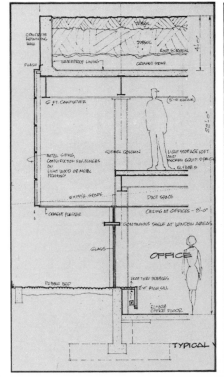
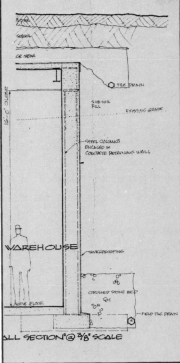

FIGS. 1.3, 1.4 *Uninsulated, leak-prone, and inappropriate, the underground design I first proposed for the Construction Fasteners job was considerate enough not to let itself be built, thus sparing me great embarrassment.*

to add any future extension to the building. The structure would have been extremely expensive, thermally disastrous, and fraught with potential ice and water problems. When I look at those drawings today I shiver a little. I had the beginnings of a commitment to an idea but I hadn't begun to think about its consequences.

At Construction Fasteners,* I have been in the unfamiliar position of having to talk a client *out* of going underground. It just hasn't been appropriate, given the site conditions and building requirements. I simply couldn't in good conscience ask this particular client on this particular site to go under. Gentle architecture doesn't necessarily mean earth cover, anyway. Underground is a good place to build when all the portents are right, but when they aren't I try to stay away from it. At Construction Fasteners, with the remaining on-site green space now at a premium, the next building addition may very well *have* to be subterranean.

Each building of any kind, built with respect for life, nudges gentle architecture forward into the unguessable future. We can never say, "Well, this is it, the perfect building." So we have, in a way, eternal life, if not for ourselves, at least for architecture—just when it seemed most in danger of dying.

Barrier-Free Buildings

It's easy to talk about living architecture, of course, when one is in full, mobile, good health, but architecture looks very different to the handicapped. Their problems were another architectural consideration to which my own commitment was very late in coming. Barrier-free design (and its easily recognized symbol) refer to the practice of making a building accessible to and safe for use by the handicapped—by all the people confined to wheelchairs and crutches, by the blind, the deaf, and those with other impairments. Stairs, toilets, elevators, drinking fountains, parking lots, doorsills, fire alarms: if these are not properly designed they can cause frightening difficulties. Many states now require that all new public buildings be made barrier-free, and it seems almost certain that at some time in the future *all* buildings will be designed in such ways that they are accessible to and safe for use by all people regardless of their physical condition. Anyone who has been even temporarily handicapped has had a glimpse of the problems faced every day by those with permanent disabilities.

FIG. 1.5

*For more information about the original Construction Fasteners building, see *Progressive Architecture, March 1971.*

My first underground building—the office in Cherry Hill, New Jersey—was full of barriers. Down a twisting flight of steps, behind a high-sill door, it was almost a textbook case of don'ts for a considerate architecture. I can't forget how embarrassed I was when a paraplegic friend from out of state stopped for a visit and had to play host to *me* in his specially equipped car out in *my* parking lot! I swore to myself I'd never design such a dumb building again. But of course I haven't always remembered. Architects get infatuated with the look of cascading stairways, zigzag spaces, stepping stones, and all the other things that so plague the less fortunate among us. Ramps take up great amounts of space, and they're often architecturally uninteresting unless done on a colossal scale. Given our architectural heritage, it's a wonder any of us even remember to think of the building features and the landscapes needed to welcome the disabled. But we must think of them, *every time*. It's the only decent way to act, and its priority is certainly higher than that of most other architectural niceties.

Buildings—even underground buildings—need not offer any barriers. There's no reason why the techniques of barrier-free design cannot apply to all structures, regardless of type. And there's no reason why they can't apply to parks, playgrounds, and pedestrian areas as well.* We think nothing, for instance, of providing barrier-free facilities in high-rise buildings. Compared to them, earthbound buildings are far easier to equip. Think of all the underground libraries and bookstores on U.S. college campuses. Most of them are already barrier-free.

Architecture isn't inherently obstructive, but out-of-date thinking is. Remember when all public buildings were made to look like Greek temples, accessible only by great flights of steps? In those days the handicapped were found behind drawn curtains at home, condemned to live apart from life. But society inches forward year by year, slowly learning from its mistakes. Those of us who are not handicapped have begun to see how blind we were and have tried to change our ways. When that change grows out of a solid commitment to and reverence for life, we may start to produce some memorable works.

---

*For information on the design of barrier-free architecture, the office of your local building inspector will at least be able to name a source in your state. Architects, of course, can get up-to-date information through their professional organizations.

CHAPTER TWO

Reverence for Life

I'm sure I heard about chlorophyll and photosynthesis when I was in school, but I don't believe they ever struck me as having any more importance than, say, the Declaration of Independence—or geometry. I doubt if they were even intended to. They were simply part of the stuff I had to learn in order to graduate. No one ever impressed upon me—or upon anyone else, apparently, judging from the state of things—the astonishing priority held by the green plants of the third planet: *priority number one.*

Take away all governments and armies, take away all businesses and industries, take away all communications; take away cars, houses, cities, hospitals, schools and libraries; take away electricty, clothes, medicine, and police; take away everything, in fact, but the green plants, and most of us would survive. But take away the plants and we would all die. That's how important they are.

Now, wouldn't you think that something that important—that vital—would have been communicated to the architects and engineers of America at some time during their education? Wouldn't you think that the value of land and the health of plants, each more precious than gold, would have been made the two top considerations by anyone about to tamper with the surface of the earth? You'd think so, all right, but in all the talk about planning and environment those central facts are almost never heard.

Green plants turn sunlight into food and fuel. They take inedible earth minerals and water and carbon dioxide, and, holding them up to the sun, give us food and fuel and oxygen in return. Green plants are all that keep the soil from washing away.

Now take a look at what *we* do. Everything we build fails. It doesn't collapse or explode or melt, but it kills all the land it touches, from the mine to the site.

Few construction practices today are based on reverence for life, but the *next* architecture of America will have to be. Its central rule will be this: improve the land when you build, or don't build there. Then we'll be forced to revive the most devastated of sites first. Slums. Worn-out farmland. Strip mines. Old parking lots. They're the kinds of places on and in which to build, and the results can be glorious—a whole new architecture in which you won't be quite sure where the land ends and the buildings begin.

Freedom of expression under really tight restrictions will give our cities character again. They'll not only be healthy, and healthful, they'll be beautiful, too. A wind-twisted tree growing out of a crack in the rock is a far more moving expression of life than is the same kind of tree rising monotonously from the well-watered rows of a nursery. An ancient city speaks to the poet and the artist in us because it has that same life-expression as the gnarled tree. It grew under natural restraints we thought we could escape forever. That's why our cities and suburbs look no more interesting than the tree-rows in the nursery. That's why our cities and suburbs have failed. We've created so much convenience and ease we've turned ourselves into an artificial people, with artificial values, who live precariously far from the roots of life. If you don't believe it, just listen to what most people are talking about. Look at what most of us are buying at the supermarket.

The Empty City

I used to wonder what would happen to the world if all the people were to disappear. In my imagination, I arranged this by slipping something into the water supply, and painlessly killing us. Nowadays, having mellowed a bit, I simply send us all off into a pleasant sort of limbo from which we can watch the miracle of regeneration take place. The empty city is a theme already overworked by film writers, but they always choose to see it as disaster; the late-night movies all seem to have been made before Earth Day.

Take the Empire State Building, for instance. From what cause might the first of its windows be shattered? A hurricane? A migrating bird? Charlton Heston? It doesn't matter; the point is that once the first pane was broken, life would begin to reawaken the silent corridors, as birds and then insects and seedlings—along with all the colonies of parasites to which they are hosts—began to set up housekeeping in what from then onward, forever, would be wilderness again, and the famous old building would accelerate its currently imperceptible march toward the bottom of the sea. The timetables, of course, are unknown to us, but surely, long before the Great Collapse of the Empire State Building, trees and flowers would have begun to grow from hundreds of its windows, there above the new forests of Thirty-Fourth Street.

Or take Broadway: when would the first tree seedling sprout from all its lifeless asphalt? Probably sooner than you'd think; I saw a blade of grass growing there last summer. That was pure optimism, of course: nature taking her usual million-to-one gamble, never knowing when The Man would finally go away and let life return to the city.

And when do you suppose the last bumper sticker would finally peel and fall from the last rusting Chevy, and wild flowers spring from its grille? Long before all the nukes had ruptured, and all the nerve-gas tanks disolved. Each time another drum of pesticide, or petroleum, or God-knows-what other noxious chemical, now so trustingly stored all over the world, had rusted through, the new wilderness would suffer a heartrending setback locally, but the health of nature, in general, would continue to improve. Within a month after the great human exodus had occurred, the smoky skies that now cover North America would be almost clear again.

It never ceases to amaze me that, each night, the TV weather forecaster can plot the pressure systems that are moving across the country, watch others move off the map into the Atlantic, and never once wonder where they go, or how they so quickly rid themselves of their vile freight before winging back, a few weeks later, fresh from Siberia or Canada. Today's cool breeze may be nothing more than last month's cold snap the second time around, but, if it is, the TV meteorologists won't tell us so. To them no highs or lows exist until they reach the studio map.

Within the first month after the human exodus, many rivers would become drinkable again, putting to lie all that "cost of clean water" nonsense. And in less than a decade, all the rats in all the slums would have been brought back under control by their own natural enemies.

There's an immense lesson in all this, a lesson we continue to disregard in spite of the daily reminders all around us. Near my home, a park maintenance building stands in an area of eroding subsoil. Right in the center of that minidesert, a sewer line overflowed and streaked the lifeless earth with gobs of melted paper and sewage. For two weeks no one bothered to clean up the mess, and then, sure enough, fresh spears of bright green grass began to grow from every inch of subsoil touched by the brownish flood. Dead land had suddenly been made fit for life again, after just a single dose of the stuff we use to kill rivers.

But the lesson goes unlearned.

New York!

I was 11 years old when my father first took me to New York. We were two yokels from the deep south (of New Jersey) who arrived at Penn Station with great expectations and were not disappointed. We couldn't have been more impressed if we'd stepped into the Land of Oz. Our trip must have occurred in the spring of 1937 because I associate it with the time of the Hindenburg disaster. It never occurred to us that all around us we were seeing the seeds of another disaster, the environmental one of New York today. We must be forgiven, though, as must everyone else, on the grounds of ignorance; we didn't know any better then.

Twenty-seven years later I was asked to design a pavilion for the World's Fair in the same city, and I approached the job with most of my childhood awe of New York still solidly intact. I can still remember the high on which I rode to the grand opening. President Johnson was there, flags were flying, and long lines of people were waiting in the cold April drizzle to see *my* building! I was sure I'd given the world something as near architectural perfection as man could devise in that bright new year of 1964; great cantilevered roofs, reflecting pools, Wrightian ramps, a single repeating geometric theme, and lovely gardens with big trees.

It's a sad thing to have to grow up in a hurry, especially if it doesn't happen until you're 38 years old. That's when it happened to me, not, by a long shot, all in one blinding flash, although it seemed abrupt enough at the time. As I toured those fairgrounds I made depressing discoveries about my building, about architecture generally, and about myself. I lost my innocence in Flushing Meadow, and nothing's seemed quite the same since.

Suddenly my architectural gem was just another part of the vast, dying city all around it. I opened my eyes and for the first time really saw all the fair's wonder buildings. A few were quite beautiful, but, when it rained, every one of them—all those acres of phony, throw-away architecture— shed torrents of precious rainwater. For the first time in my life I asked, and was told, where all the sewage was going. It was bad news, all of it, worse than I'd dreamed: a supernova in a teacup, an event already half forgotten, and at what a price! Wasted materials, wasted energy, wasted years, wasted land! It had never occurred to me before that land had higher uses, that the light blazing out of a city at night was nothing but a massive waste of power, or that New York itself had been in far better health the day it was sold for 24 dollars.

As I began to look back over all my other works, at all the factories and offices and churches I'd produced, I found that I'd already paved to death over 50 acres of the American land. Those 50 acres had been wiped out in order to provide a single species with shelter.

Don't get me wrong; many of those buildings were reasonably attractive and well landscaped. They were widely accepted, and many of them got good exposure in the architectural press. But the devastation and waste they caused far outweighed their better qualities.

FIG. 2.1 (above) *Job number one: in 1953, four days after my architectural registration took effect, I was asked to do the Church of Christ in Collingswood, New Jersey. I was so new to the profession I didn't know what a building code was, and I thought architecture was primarily an exercise in geometry; but the building won an AIA award, and cost only 9 dollars per square foot. (Artog)*

FIG. 2.2 (left) *Job number 21: my first architectural office, Cherry Hill, New Jersey, 1955. It's so heavily landscaped it looks as if it grew there, but its looks are deceptive: it wastes energy, repels rainwater, and paves over land just as all other conventional buildings do. (Artog)*

By 1964, my lifetime expanse of paving and roofs, dotted across a half-dozen states, had repelled over 500 million gallons of rainwater, water that had fallen toward what should have been soft, moist, living earth—and a season of usefulness. Instead, it was sent coursing down drainage ditches and storm sewers, eroding its way to the sea. And now, over 15 years later, those same 50 acres—plus, I'm bound to admit, a few acres more—have moved well into the *billions*-of-gallons-repelled category, from which heights they will continue to set new records, year after year, until the day on which they are at last demolished.

Wasted rainwater is only part of the story; there's all that sewage, too, sewage piped to inadequate treatment plants, all those tons of topsoil eroded away, all the building materials wasted, and all the fuels burned to replace the heat that continually leaks through those inadequate walls and roofs. In a saner society I might have been jailed for such things, but having done only what I was expected to do, I was instead invited to become a Jaycee, a Rotarian, and a member of the American Institute of Architects.

They say there's no zealot quite like a convert, and I proved it, right after my World's Fair years, by speaking out with complete authority on all my new discoveries. Little escaped my wrath. That others had discovered the same things years earlier was lost upon me. I had found the way.

Not long after my rise to grace, I called the entire office staff—all seven of them—into the conference room and announced that from then on I would do nothing but earth-and-tree-covered buildings. My clients soon got wind of my vow and began staying away in droves, shrinking my staff to five, to three, and then to one. It worked no hardship on the staff; they all got better-paying jobs right away. And I never missed a meal, but the experience began to teach me that talking was not the same as doing, as actually producing something; and that the reeducation of myself was going to be a long, slow process.

I made, and still manage to make, a disheartening number of mistakes in the name of land-respect. However, there was an encouraging number of small successes as well: the factory at Reading, buildings with heat-saving insulations, landscapes that needed little watering or maintenance, underground roofs with really good waterproofings, and solar heating; each of these pointed a direction leading me to the discovery that, far off at the end of the road down which I was stumbling, there already existed a near-perfect system called nature, that had, over endless eons of trial and error, already evolved many of the very structures and processes we so badly needed.

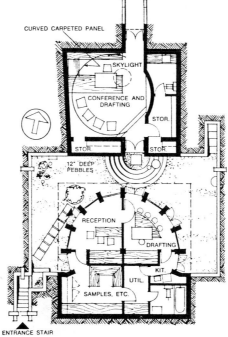

CURVED CARPETED PANEL

SKYLIGHT

CONFERENCE AND
DRAFTING

STOR.

STOR.

STOR.

12" DEEP
PEBBLES

RECEPTION

DRAFTING

KIT.

UTIL.

SAMPLES, ETC.

ENTRANCE STAIR

FIG. 2.3 (above) *Job number 426; My second architectural office and my first underground building, it taught me a great deal about that kind of construction, and paved the way to other earth-sheltered projects. Cherry Hill, N.J. 1970. (Ken Basmajian)*

FIG. 2.4 (left) *Plan of the underground office at Cherry Hill.*

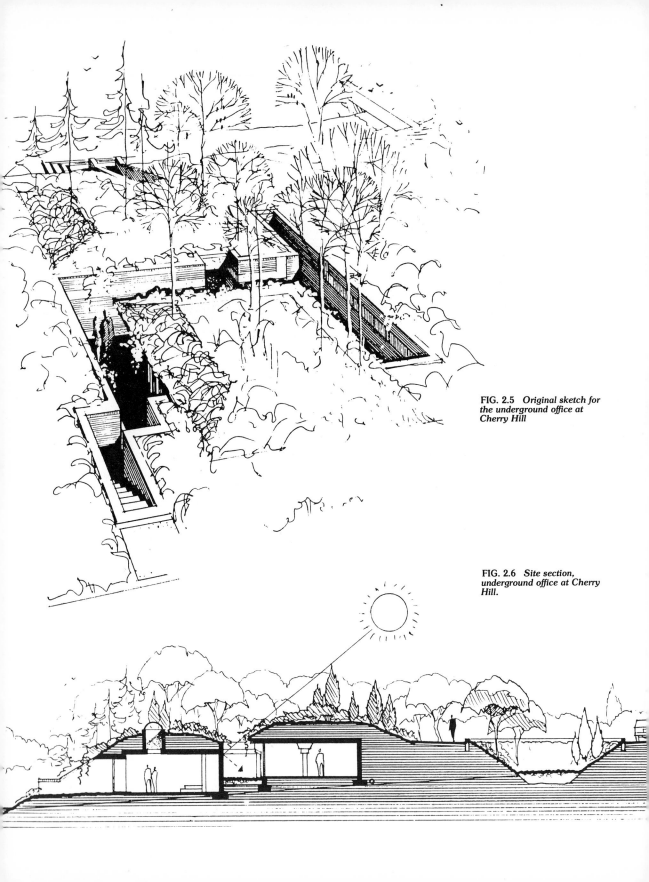

FIG. 2.5 *Original sketch for the underground office at Cherry Hill*

FIG. 2.6 *Site section, underground office at Cherry Hill.*

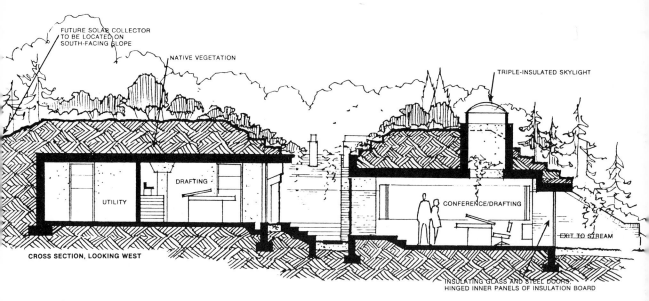

FUTURE SOLAR COLLECTOR
TO BE LOCATED ON
SOUTH-FACING SLOPE

NATIVE VEGETATION

TRIPLE-INSULATED SKYLIGHT

UTILITY

DRAFTING

CONFERENCE/DRAFTING

EXIT TO STREAM

CROSS SECTION, LOOKING WEST

INSULATING GLASS AND STEEL DOORS,
HINGED INNER PANELS OF INSULATION BOARD

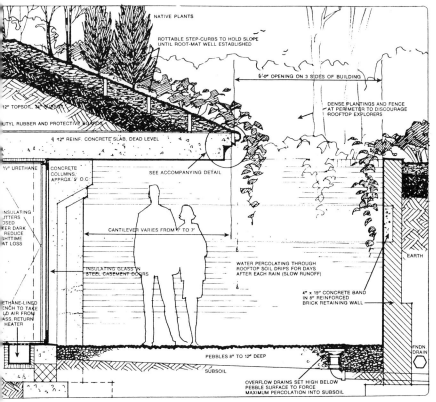

NATIVE PLANTS

ROTTABLE STEP-CURBS TO HOLD SLOPE
UNTIL ROOT-MAT WELL ESTABLISHED

6'-0" OPENING ON 3 SIDES OF BUILDING

DENSE PLANTINGS AND FENCE
AT PERIMETER TO DISCOURAGE
ROOFTOP EXPLORERS

12" TOPSOIL, 24" SUBSOIL

BUTYL RUBBER AND PROTECTIVE BOARD

4 12" REINF. CONCRETE SLAB, DEAD LEVEL

SEE ACCOMPANYING DETAIL

½" URETHANE

CONCRETE
COLUMNS:
APPROX. 9' O.C.

INSULATING
SHUTTERS
CLOSED
AFTER DARK
REDUCE
NIGHTTIME
HEAT LOSS

CANTILEVER VARIES FROM 1' TO 7'

INSULATING GLASS IN
STEEL CASEMENT DOORS

WATER PERCOLATING THROUGH
ROOFTOP SOIL DRIPS FOR DAYS
AFTER EACH RAIN (SLOW RUNOFF)

4" x 15" CONCRETE BAND
IN 8" REINFORCED
BRICK RETAINING WALL

EARTH

URETHANE-LINED
TRENCH TO TAKE
COLD AIR FROM
GLASS, RETURN
TO HEATER

PEBBLES 8" TO 12" DEEP

SUBSOIL

OVERFLOW DRAINS SET HIGH BELOW
PEBBLE SURFACE TO FORCE
MAXIMUM PERCOLATION INTO SUBSOIL

FNDN.
DRAIN

FIG. 2.7 (above) *Building section, underground office at Cherry Hill.*

FIG. 2.8 (left) *Wall sections, underground office at Cherry Hill, as published in Progressive Architecture, June 1974. Used with permission.*

FIG. 2.9 (below) *Roof detail, underground office at Cherry Hill.*

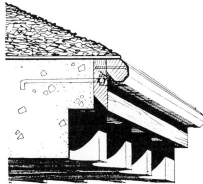

1/16" BUTYL RUBBER
ROLLED AROUND A
MULTI-CHAMFERED 3" x 3"

FORMS FOR SLAB EDGE:
6" x 6" x 3" HALF-CANS
OF SHEET METAL AND
PLYWOOD

To a visitor from a faraway planet (to borrow another overworked theme) coming back for another of Earth's regular 10,000-year check-ups, the most shocking change from the familiar cycles of ice age and warm age, a change visible from quite far out in space, would very likely be the one resulting from agriculture—vast brown areas where green had been—and its two most visible side effects, siltation and cities: muddy rivers and great, dead gridirons of brick and asphalt. To the visitor, farms would be understandable:

- Green plants turn solar energy into food.
- Man has the beginnings of intelligence, therefore
- Man must at first grow plants selectively.

But the other things, the dead rivers and the cities, would be harder to comprehend. If the very foundation of life on the blue-green planet is the film of plants that covers all the lands and seas, then why would man cover such huge areas with row after row of his wasteful dead boxes? Frank Lloyd Wright called them coffins for living, but it took the age of ecology to show us that while a building may be many things, it is first of all a destroyer of land.

Many years have passed since Jane Jacobs wrote, in her classic work on urban planners and planning,[1] about the importance of diversity to healthy neighborhoods. Her book got some nice reviews, but she stepped on the toes of too many planners who insisted on making their own mistakes. It was years before her views were widely accepted, but now our mistakes have proved her right, and her book is finally *in* . Still, Jane Jacobs didn't invent the idea of diversity. It seems to have been at the heart of all healthy and stable systems. It is certainly the key to nature's long record of success. In the natural world, a million kinds of plants and animals compete and cooperate in very complicated ways in order to survive. By contrast, cities are dead, made as they are for just one species. Suburbs are almost as bad. Saddest of all, perhaps, is the speed at which even the rural village is taking on the tired, bright plasticity of its urban and suburban cousins.

Wilderness Values
Now for the good news. I keep mentioning wilderness not because I'm a great outdoorsman nor because I'm against the idea of having cities, but because I see in the wilderness model the only way of saving the cities. Remember that what we call wilderness, or nature, is a community. If a

[1]*The Death and Life of Great American Cities,* Random House, New York, 1961.

city is a community housed in geometric structures and served by vastly sophisticated life-support systems, then wilderness can be thought of as a city as well. The difference is that wilderness works; cities no longer do. Wilderness had a flexible sort of stability over long periods of time. Wilderness lives—thrives, in fact—by using only the energy that shines upon it or blows through it each year. The inhabitants of wilderness are all fully employed. It produces its own food without sapping, as cities do, half a continent to feed its largest communities. And it recycles everything, not just a little bit of everything, but *everything!* In short, wilderness works. It had a billion-year head start over what we call civilization, a billion years to find the best way to survive here. So doesn't it seem highly unlikely that we'll ever find any totally different way to live on this same planet, under the same ground rules, and find it before all the slums get fenced, the wells run dry, and the land dies?

Wilderness supports its everlasting network of communities on what green leaves do when irradiated by sunlight. It's simple as that, only that's not so simple. In nature as in architecture, simplicity is based on great complexity.

During the past decade, when so much publicity has been given to our doubtful future on this planet, nearly all architects have come to think of themselves as environmentalists. But while "environmental" is sometimes stretched to include desperately needed low-income housing, few architects look beyond their buildings to the planetary systems into which they all must plug.

Earth Day is celebrated every April, but we see little change. The prospect of a dramatic, new land ethic coming out of Washington is not very bright. And yet the situation is by no means hopeless. Every few days or so we seem to hear of promising new developments:

- Wind power is turning electricity into easily stored hydrogen for later use in heating, cooking, and making electricity again.

- Sewerless toilets, the ones that make fertilizer out of human wastes and kitchen scraps, are being installed, challenging the insane modern practice of dropping such wastes into drinking water.

- In Massachusetts, the New Alchemists, a group of young scientists, are learning how to live almost entirely within the solar budget by using everything from windmills and bioshelters to algae tanks, fish farms, and organic gardens.

- Thousands of earth-covered homes, many of them solar-heated, are now under construction in at least thirty-seven states.

- Each year's top architectural design awards feature greater numbers of low-impact buildings and low-energy systems.

Aesthetic simplicity, which is a satisfaction to the mind, derives, when valid and profound, from inner complexity.

ROBERT VENTURI

- And in Florida, a man is teaching manufacturers to see pollution as nothing but their own private property, lost to them and illegally dumped into the public domain; to regard such wastes as the valuable resources they really are; and to make more money from good housekeeping than from government "pollution-control" programs that do nothing but legalize sky dumping and river killing.

The list grows all the time. There's a sizable army of both pros and amateurs at work, eager to prove that the right way is not only possible but sometimes even cheaper. The moment they make their case, the immense power of the courts will start to help. No longer will juries be confused by self-serving cries of "Too expensive," "Not so fast," or "You're eliminating jobs!" Once the jurors see their first *low-cost* solar-heated building, or their first economical resource-recovery project, there will be no further argument. They'll say, "This guy did it; you must, too."

The implications of all this to the cities are huge. And it's not even necessary to wait until all the verdicts are in. Much of the hardware and the know-how are available today. The basic experiments have already been done.

Coexistence

Picture the great tiered garden levels that will rise above what are now depressingly lifeless, energy-wasting, water-repelling rooftops, each stepped-back tier a floor overlooking terraces of wildflowers, trees, ponds, and gardens. Organic wastes will be composted automatically and then spread on the rooftop soils, constantly enriching them. Streets and parking lots will be tucked away underneath the buildings, down where cars belong, leaving the sunny green rooftops for people and other animals to use. These won't be the potted-plant landscapes you see around penthouses or atop so many of today's so-called underground buildings. These will be honest-to-God fields with deep topsoil and mulch above well-drained, well-insulated roofs with hundred-year waterproofings: living land meant to stay that way for generations regardless of the occupancy changes below it. Not only can shops and offices be built that way, but factories and hospitals and housing for all income groups can too, each room with its window on the living world visible just beyond the glass.

A New Jersey shopping center advertises everlasting springtime weather indoors, regardless of the outdoor season. It was built in the spring of 1961, and, sure enough, the advertisements are true: that same 1961 springtime weather is still in there, enriched, after all these years, with body odors, hairspray, indigestion, smoke, diaper accidents, solvents, pesticides, and ten thousand other goodies from the world of science. The giant complex of shops and stores was provided with reasonably effective ventilation equipment for the introduction of fresh air, but since it costs far more to heat or cool incoming outdoor air than it does to recirculate stale air, the dollar argument has won, every year.

Megastructures

I think of that shopping center, unfairly perhaps, whenever I see pictured the domed-over cities proposed by R. Buckminster Fuller, or the desert megastructures of Paolo Soleri. My skepticism isn't based on any lack of respect for those two gifted men. It's based on what I see happening whenever budgets collide with recommended practices. Hard-pressed building managers throw procedures out the window when the squeeze is on. That's why a gentler, smaller-scaled, decentralized architecture, with its emphasis on natural systems—natural ventilation, natural lighting, natural treatment of wastes, natural heating and air conditioning—has more appeal to me. Rather than get stranded by an elevator failure or a bomb scare or a strike on the 300th floor of a megastructure, the inhabitant of a terraced garden block would make his exit to the out-of-doors, naturally, via the landscaped rooftop just outside the windows of his particular level. The idea of it all, of course, is not only the creation of an architecture that's gentler on the land, but also the creation of a new life for the people of the cities. Most of us still have no idea how utterly dependent we are on green leaves and sunlight, and must depend, for our source of information, on what the fifth-graders can tell us at the dinner table. Still, the facts of life must surely be tucked away in our heads somewhere, just waiting to be awakened.

Out on the lecture circuit, I sometimes forget to describe the way in which I see all this coming about, and my forgetfulness always generates questions:

"You can't put these gardens on the roofs of existing buildings, can you?"

"Would we have to abandon our cities in order to do all this?"

"I don't see how this can be done for any amount less than the national debt."

When I remember to describe the process involved in building the new cities I never get such questions.

As I see it, all we need do is *start,* start with a tiny row house, if necessary, or a doughnut shop or a fruit stand. One by one. It's the way the quiet city got destroyed. It's the way we'll replace the noisy one. Larger projects will grow out of the experience accumulated on all the small ones.

Factory-Made Houses

Most buildings are still built on the spot, piece by piece, just as they were a hundred or a thousand years ago, but big changes are coming, and our real test may not even begin for a few years more, when the factory-made buildings now being developed begin to flood the market. If we've learned nothing at all from the lessons of the times, we'll scatter those prefabs across the land in a binge of littering like nothing we've ever seen before, killing everything in their paths.

But who's to say we can't start to use our heads, and do with all those automated wonders the only thing we *can* do and still survive? Set them undercover, just out of the rain, on permanent terraces below great sheltering ledges of landscaped earth. Protect them with forested shelves designed to last for centuries, so we can come and go, plug and unplug the buildings as their usefulness changes, reuse and recycle every component without further destroying the land.

It will be the near-perfect marriage of architecture and technology, of life and the machine; great vine-draped sun courts in man-made landscapes, gardens descending to "street" level, or ascending the slopes of hills, cities crusted with lichens and memories, sheltering the bright new spaces, architecture no longer at war with the world. Living room.

I no longer blame Detroit so much, or the oil men or the chemical companies; it's all us damned designers out here accommodating every known ecological mistake in the name of environmental design, building cities and suburbs that need too many cars and too much power, and make too much waste.

FIG. 2.10

Unpreparedness

Back in the sixties, Narendra Juneja, an associate of ecologist Ian McHarg's at the University of Pennsylvania, surprised me by predicting that future historians would probably not blame public apathy or political spinelessness for our environmental crisis as much as they would the unpreparedness of the experts. He foresaw a sudden demand for answers—for specifics, hardware, details—that would catch those of us in the construction industry unawares. Now his prediction has begun to come true. Where in your town can you buy reliable, low-cost solar heating systems? Does your neighborhood heating contractor offer them and guarantee their performance? Are waterless tolilets available where you live? Have they even been approved for use there yet? Other than recommend better insulation or offer the address of the nearest recycling center, too many of us find ourselves at a loss when members of public ask what they can do, particularly in construction. That they want to do something is obvious; they and I are fast becoming aware that the only treasure we'll ever have is this incredible ball beneath our feet.

Wilderness developed myriad responses to the land challenge. Appropriateness is their common quality. Wilderness would never build a Cape Cod cottage in Arizona, but I know of an architect who did. Nature's way of dealing with land, with structures, and with communities can be outlined in the simplest of ways (as I am about to outline it), or it can be metered and monitored down to a particle of a cell and up to the pulsing of the cosmos. Each of us studies at his own level, and each study offers powerful hints, if not downright instructions, as to the ways in which we should meet similar challenges when *we* build. Within a few miles of each of us, right now, acres and acres of land lie open, stripped bare, ready for construction, choking nearby valleys with silt, and driving all the wildlife away. At this very moment, all those thousands of acres are ready to undergo, in the name of architecture, even greater indignities, and in Washington, nobody is saying "stop!"

We can all agree, I suppose, that the right attitude, in confronting a building site, is to leave it better than we found it, but who can weigh a badly needed new hospital, say, against the forest it will replace, and be sure of his ground? We just aren't equipped to make such decisions, a fact easily proved simply by looking around us. But just imagine a hospital that was *itself* actually healthy, alive; a building that was a hospital and a forest as well!

In the few generations since we left the land we've lost all awareness of the people-to-land relationship. It still takes about three thousand years to produce a giant redwood tree in spite of the fact that it now takes only three minutes to kill one. It still takes about a century to build an inch of natural topsoil in spite of the fact that we can now bulldoze acres of it away in a matter of hours. We're utterly out of step, and nature can't be made to hurry, no matter what you may hear about those fast-growing new strains the lumber industry likes to brag about. *Our* rhythms are adjustable; nature's aren't.

We must swallow our pride and begin to learn something from a blade of grass or a cockroach. It will be a small step for us, but—how does it go?—a giant step for architecture. The point of course, is that there *are* great standards against which we can assess anything from an eroded site to a shopping center—or a city.

Here is a 15-point value scale on which sites and buildings and cities can be rated.[3] Wilderness gets a perfect score, + 1500.

[3]These graphs were first published in *Progressive Architecture,* March, 1971.

Nothing else ever rates quite so high.

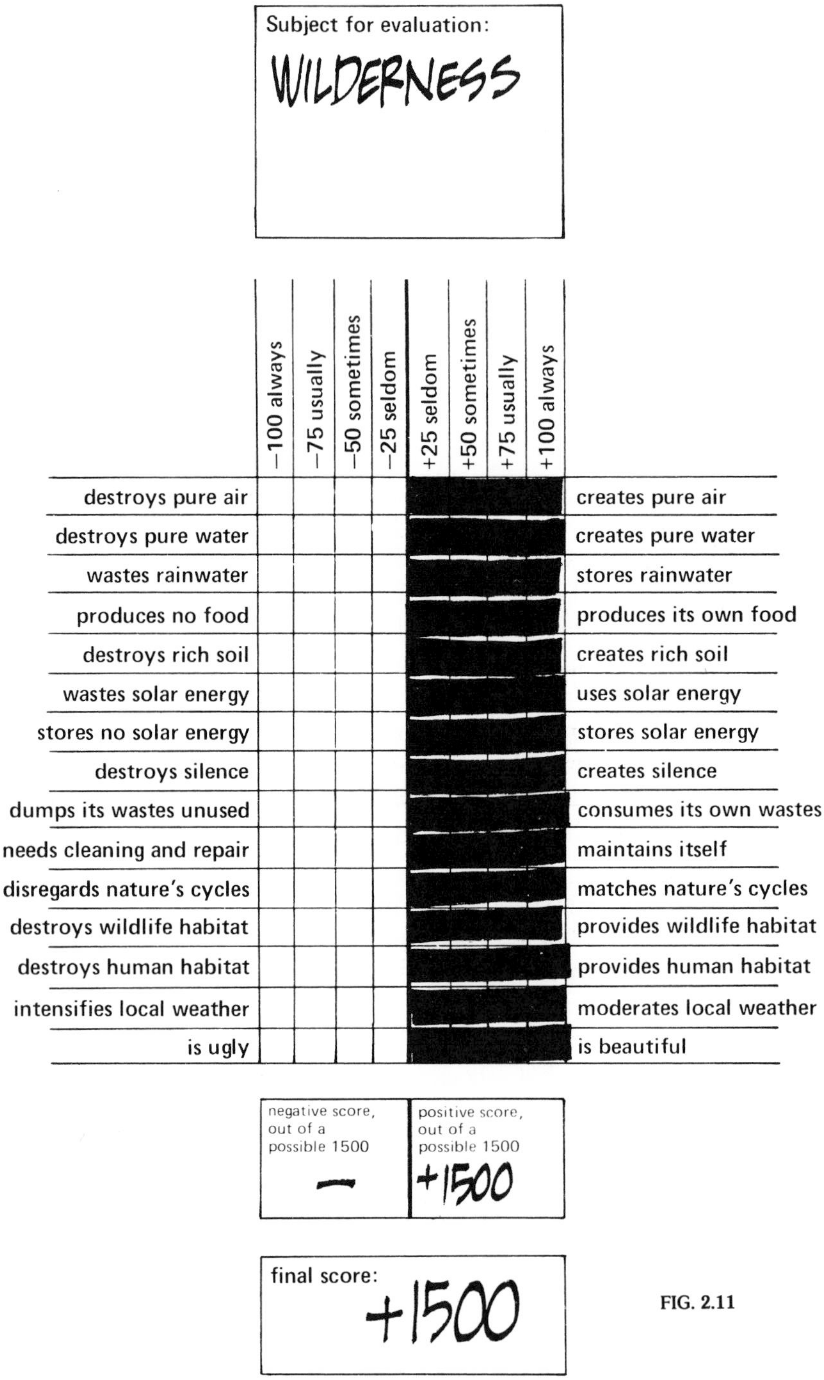

Subject for evaluation: WILDERNESS									

	−100 always	−75 usually	−50 sometimes	−25 seldom	+25 seldom	+50 sometimes	+75 usually	+100 always	
destroys pure air									creates pure air
destroys pure water									creates pure water
wastes rainwater									stores rainwater
produces no food									produces its own food
destroys rich soil									creates rich soil
wastes solar energy									uses solar energy
stores no solar energy									stores solar energy
destroys silence									creates silence
dumps its wastes unused									consumes its own wastes
needs cleaning and repair									maintains itself
disregards nature's cycles									matches nature's cycles
destroys wildlife habitat									provides wildlife habitat
destroys human habitat									provides human habitat
intensifies local weather									moderates local weather
is ugly									is beautiful

negative score, out of a possible 1500	positive score, out of a possible 1500
—	+1500

final score:
+1500

FIG. 2.11

Eroded farmland gets a lower rating.

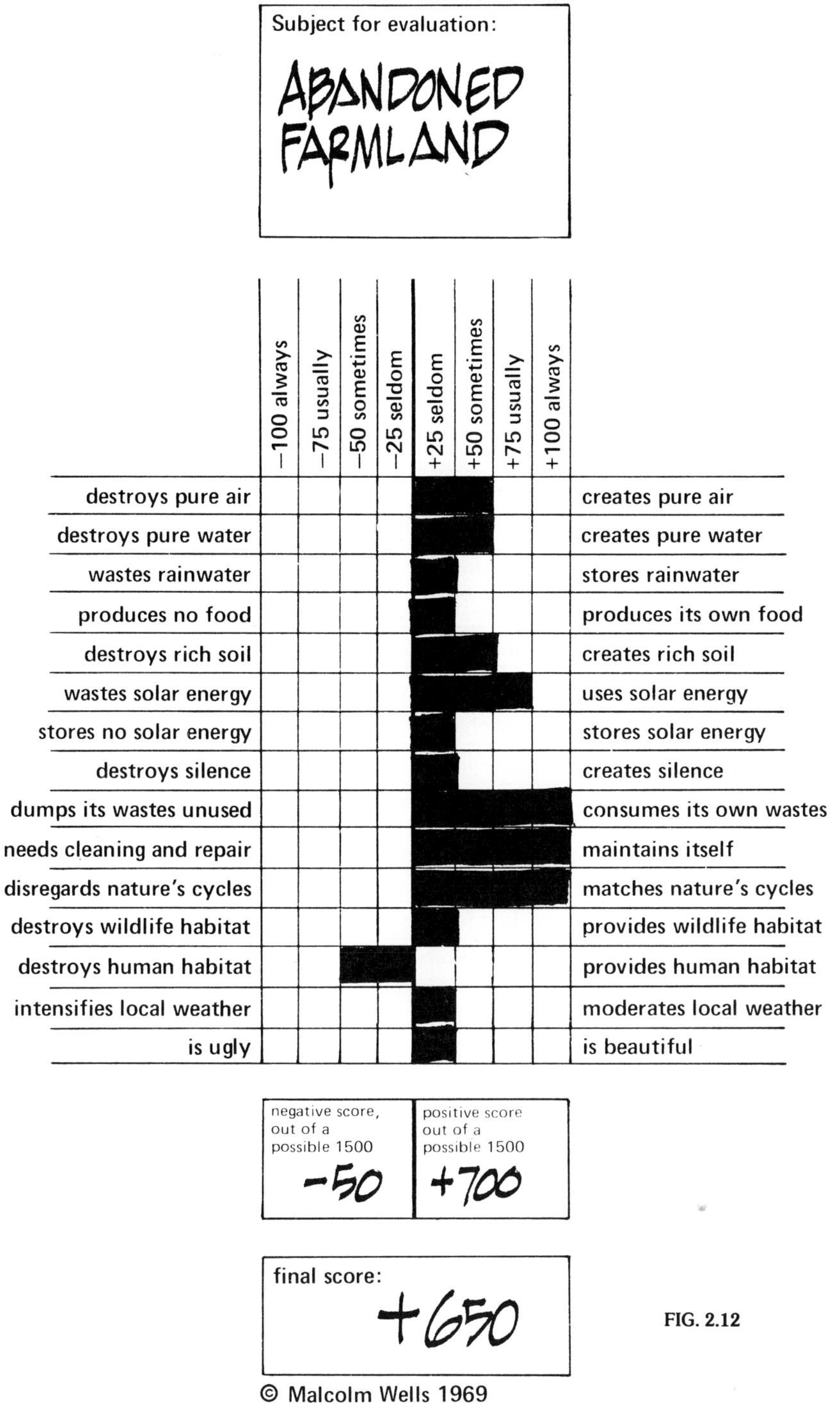

Subject for evaluation:

ABANDONED FARMLAND

	−100 always	−75 usually	−50 sometimes	−25 seldom	+25 seldom	+50 sometimes	+75 usually	+100 always	
destroys pure air					■				creates pure air
destroys pure water					■				creates pure water
wastes rainwater					■				stores rainwater
produces no food				■	■				produces its own food
destroys rich soil					■				creates rich soil
wastes solar energy					■	■			uses solar energy
stores no solar energy						■			stores solar energy
destroys silence						■			creates silence
dumps its wastes unused					■	■			consumes its own wastes
needs cleaning and repair					■	■	■		maintains itself
disregards nature's cycles					■	■			matches nature's cycles
destroys wildlife habitat						■			provides wildlife habitat
destroys human habitat				■					provides human habitat
intensifies local weather					■				moderates local weather
is ugly					■				is beautiful

negative score, out of a possible 1500	positive score out of a possible 1500
−50	+700

final score:
+650

FIG. 2.12

And when you start rating architecture, the scores really tumble. The dazzling new research center on the hill just outside of town scores *minus* 750.

Subject for evaluation:

	−100 always	−75 usually	−50 sometimes	−25 seldom	+25 seldom	+50 sometimes	+75 usually	+100 always	
destroys pure air			■	■					creates pure air
destroys pure water	■	■	■						creates pure water
wastes rainwater	■	■	■	■					stores rainwater
produces no food	■	■	■	■					produces its own food
destroys rich soil			■	■					creates rich soil
wastes solar energy			■	■					uses solar energy
stores no solar energy	■	■	■	■					stores solar energy
destroys silence				■					creates silence
dumps its wastes unused	■	■	■	■					consumes its own wastes
needs cleaning and repair		■	■	■					maintains itself
disregards nature's cycles		■	■	■					matches nature's cycles
destroys wildlife habitat					■				provides wildlife habitat
destroys human habitat					■	■			provides human habitat
intensifies local weather				■					moderates local weather
is ugly					■				is beautiful

negative score, out of a possible 1500	positive score, out of a possible 1500
−850	+100

final score:

−750

FIG. 2.13

And Manhattan just about hits bottom with its score of *minus* 1100.

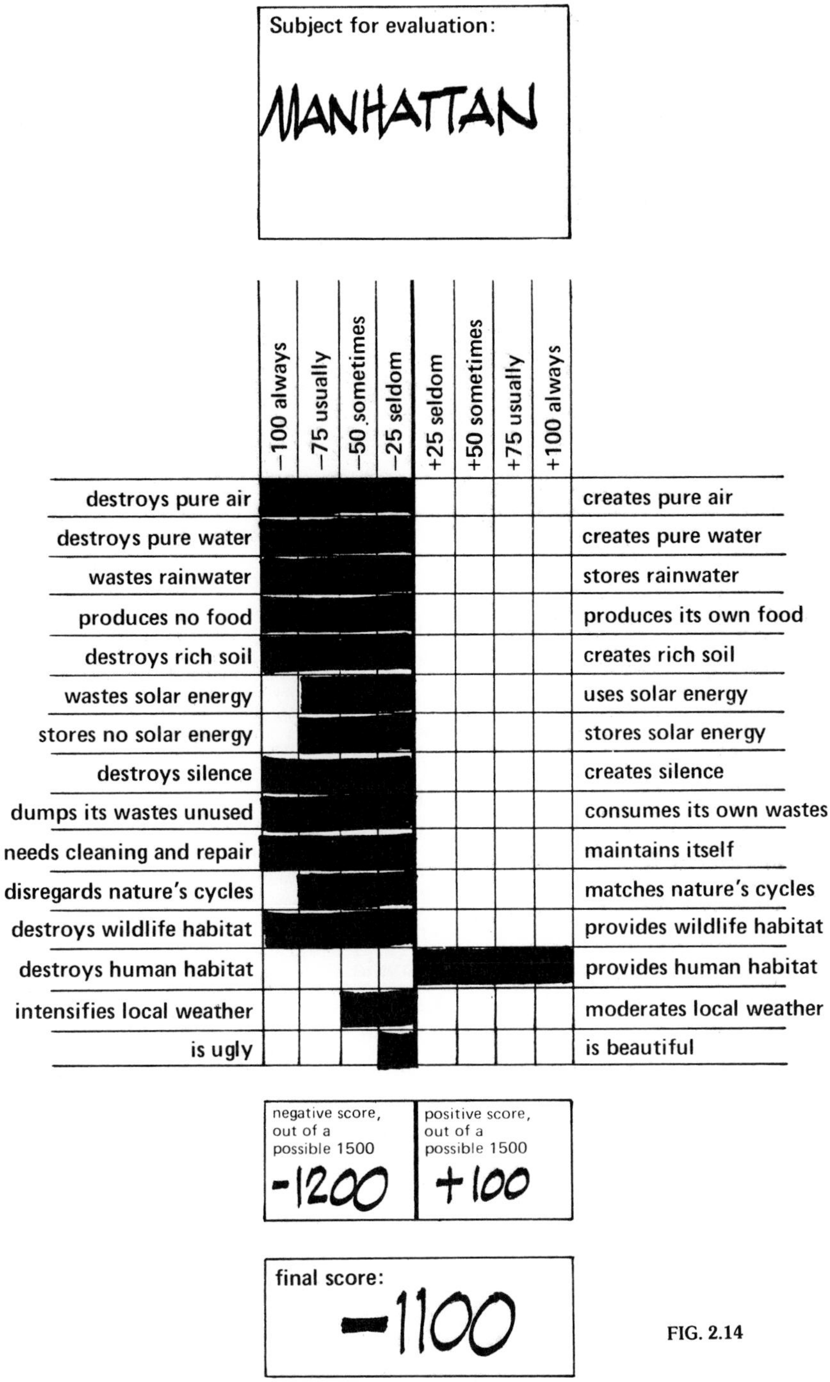

Subject for evaluation:

MANHATTAN

	-100 always	-75 usually	-50 sometimes	-25 seldom	+25 seldom	+50 sometimes	+75 usually	+100 always	
destroys pure air	■								creates pure air
destroys pure water	■								creates pure water
wastes rainwater	■								stores rainwater
produces no food	■								produces its own food
destroys rich soil	■								creates rich soil
wastes solar energy		■							uses solar energy
stores no solar energy		■							stores solar energy
destroys silence	■								creates silence
dumps its wastes unused	■								consumes its own wastes
needs cleaning and repair	■								maintains itself
disregards nature's cycles		■							matches nature's cycles
destroys wildlife habitat	■								provides wildlife habitat
destroys human habitat						■			provides human habitat
intensifies local weather			■						moderates local weather
is ugly				■					is beautiful

negative score, out of a possible 1500	positive score, out of a possible 1500
-1200	+100

final score:

-1100

FIG. 2.14

© Malcolm Wells 1969

Wherever it is, your town is little or no better. There's nothing wrong with Manhattan that a good dose of life won't cure.

This book is not primarily about social or cultural values, although it's obvious that they and life values are intertwined. The wilderness graph ratings tell us far more than would at first appear about our degree of physical success as a species. (It's abysmal.) The only good that can be said about it is that there seems to be no way to go but up, and we can take it one step at a time. There's no need to try for a perfect score. We'd never make it, anyway.

With wilderness as our guide we have a stable goal in sight, one that won't be replaced next week, or by the next Congress. All we have to do is make sure the rating of each site is higher after we've "improved" it. That alone could be one of the most tremendous steps ever taken in the history of architecture.

A Wilderness-Based Checklist for Design and Construction

Be certain that the project

1. *Creates pure air.* First of all, stop dumping the products of combusion into my sky. Then plant every possible outdoor inch with native trees, shrubs, vines, and grasses. Or, better yet, let it all go wild; let natural selection handle the design. Deep mulch, and peace, are all that are needed in most parts of the United States. Left alone, under a protective, moisture-holding layer, the earth will usually spring back to life again. There's no better way to create oxygen, to absorb CO_2, or to filter smoky air. Tight little dot-dot-dot landscapes (featuring exotic plants that require constant watering and fertilizer) are wasteful, expensive, and inappropriate.

2. *Creates pure water.* Everything above applies here with equal force. Life values can't be separated into unrelated categories. In addition to giving plants their freedom, however, vast improvements must be made in our attitudes toward rainwater. Many paved and roofed areas should of course be put underground. Short of that, the use of porous paving, percolation beds, and retention basins must become second nature. Remember that every storm drainage pipe is the admission of a failure somewhere upstream and that lawn mowers, insecticides, and weed-killers work directly against the life force.

3. *Stores rainwater.* The best place to store rainwater is in the earth. If the soil where you live is impervious to water it's all the more important to hold the rain in deep surface layers of mulch, releasing it slowly to the plants and to the watercourses it feeds.

There are many specific situations in which our synthetic environments are superior to nature's. But this is no adequate basis for the mechanistic conclusion that we "don't need nature anymore." On the contrary, with the complexity of modern building we need nature more than ever before. It is not a question of air conditioning versus sea-breezes, of fluorescent tubes versus the sun. It is rather the necessity for integrating the two at the highest possible level. . . . To intervene effectively in the situation in which we find ourselves —that is to construct a truly effective 'third environment' for individual and social life —both architect and urban designer require a much deeper understanding of the terrestrial environment than they commonly display. For the quality which most characterizes all contemporary architectural and urbanistic activity everywhere in the world today is a profound misunderstanding of ecological realities. This misunderstanding is, in turn,

4. *Produces its own food.* You may not be able to feed a whole family with the food grown directly on a small site, let alone on a rooftop, but homegrown food can't be beat, and a peach plucked fresh from a fourth-level rooftop orchard is bound to be far better than one that was trucked a thousand miles. Considering the world food crisis we should be raising *food,* and not shopping centers, on our best farmland.

5. *Creates rich soil.* Topsoil is alive; don't destory it! A few bags of 5-10-5 are not the answer. Soil-building ground covers, earthworms, composted organic wastes, and mulch will restore ailing land to healthful life again. Sun power makes it happen.

6. *Uses solar energy.* We all use solar energy every day. Because of the sun, the coldest January day is far, far warmer than the −273° C of absolute zero. Wood, coal, oil, gas—even sugar—give us their stored sunlight on demand. But the burning of fuels turns the skies brown, and fuels have higher uses, anyway. Properly insulated buildings can often be heated by using nothing but sunlight.

7. *Stores solar energy.* When we start to use solar energy on a massive scale, the green world can once again begin laying up for the future more of the fossil treasures we have now virtually depleted. In order to use solar energy we must store it, whether overnight or over winter, as nature has learned to do. As the high-tech side of the solar industry gets more and more complicated the low-tech side gets simpler. You can imagine which side will require fewer expensive service calls.

8. *Creates silence.* Cities can be silent. Why isn't silence a basic human right? We seem to be able to tolerate anything, but look at us: a neurotic generation. Is there a connection? Dense plantings, soft surfaces, non-parallel walls, vibration eliminators, insulation, and machines located underground can give us utter peace and privacy, even in the busiest parts of town.

9. *Consumes its own wastes.* In wilderness, everything *is* and then *isn't* and then *is* again. Now the city must work that magic, too. Ocean-dumping, "sanitary" landfills, sewage—shame on us! It's not only the poisoning of the world, it's the *waste!* Have you ever done a survey of total wastes and resources for a building you were about to build? If you have, you are most rare. Do it; there are ways, right now, to capture and reuse almost every resource that goes into a building—or into its occupants.

10. *Maintains itself.* Sunlight, water, and ice, not to mention smoky skies, are rough on building materials. Protect exposed surfaces in every way possible. Redwood ages gracefully, and aluminum holds up well (away from salt air), but consider their other costs: stump-covered mountainsides and huge power waste. Building with dead materials as we do,

characterized by two sorts of error. One is a lack of comprehension of the absolute interrelatedness of all the component elements of the natural environment —an interdependence which makes it impossible to manipulate one factor without setting in motion a complex chain reaction that usually extends far beyond the individual designer's sphere of action. The other error is the consistent tendency of modern architects and engineers grossly to underestimate the magnitude of the natural forces of the environment; or contrariwise, grossly to overestimate the magnitude of manmade capacities at their disposal.

While we cannot expect architects and urban designers to be also meteorologists and climatologists, we might at least demand that they have a general understanding of the ecological systems which they are constantly called up to manipulate in one way or another.

JAMES MARSTON FITCH

we're forced to compromise, so compromise well. Underground buildings are ideal in this regard, hiding their skins from the damaging elements. Mowing, repainting, and reroofing can almost be forgotten when earth architecture is the theme.

11. *Matches nature's pace.* Our twenty-year cycles of construction bear no relation to life's grand, century-by-century pace. We must move toward the use of permanent architectural shells within which we can make our restless changes without damaging the land around or above them. The rhythm of the seasons is part of our heritage whether we like it or not. The current way of dealing with it is to fight, but that's one fight we cannot win.

12. *Provides wildlife habitat.* Let the old first families move back into town. Whole communities of wildlife—the kind we now expect to see only in zoos—will return and set up housekeeping at our doorsteps once we get the asphalt out of our blood. Wild creatures don't have to be invited twice; provide the right habitat and they'll appear as if by magic.

13. *Provides human habitat.* This has been almost the only goal of architecture for centuries. A wider view of the world now seems to be in order.

14. *Moderates climate and weather.* Nothing tames storms like living plant growth. In the forest, a gale is only a sound in the treetops. Underground, a cold wave is unknown. Dense groves of maintenance-free plants (all right: weeds, if that's what you want to call them!) above an underground parking lot will shelter the asphalt, moderating its temperature extremes until we learn to do better. Mounds and ponds will further temper the gales that paving and city canyons breed.

15. *. . . and is beautiful.* When architecture draws its lessons from the wild, beauty will no longer have to be applied. That's an empty exercise. Organic rightness—appropriateness—will repair the broken connection between architecture and its roots.

CHAPTER THREE

Design Theory

Why is it that almost every architect can recognize and appreciate beauty in the natural world and yet so often fail to endow his own work with it? Most modern buildings are something less than inspiring, sometimes far less. But when architects bring photographs back from trips they often exhibit great sensitivity to composition, color, and proportion. What's wrong? Why do even the worst of the picture snappers among those architects know, for instance, that this:

Esthetic judgment constitutes the quintessential level of human consciousness. . . . To be genuinely effective, a building must conform to esthetic as well as physiological standards of performance.

JAMES MARSTON FITCH

is better than this:

and this

better than this?

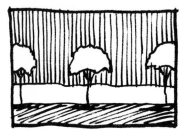

Still, almost without exception, those same architects' buildings are more likely to come out looking like this

than this.

And when environmental priorities get added to the mix, the results get even worse.

Why is it that so much of the new, less destructive architecture is even uglier, more poorly proportioned, than that of conventional design? Some say it's because architects who are interested in, say, solar heating and waterless toilets tend to be technicians at heart rather than designers. Others put the blame on the profession's lack of design experience under the new priorities. But those reasons aren't convincing: many new movements generate their purest and freshest expressions right at the start.

The fault probably lies with our education. How do you turn someone into an artist? It's doubtful that schools can ever be expected to do it. They can offer a wide exposure to great ideas, to great buildings, but the art seed seems to be planted in only a gifted few at birth and germinates in ways we cannot understand. Perhaps the best that schools of architecture can do is present the widest range of experience to the potential designer, teach him the environmental consequences of his craft, and then hope for the best. As a result we might at least have *harmless* ugly buildings instead of all these harmful ones, and the artists among us could put more solid foundations under their works.

Before the modern movement came along, architects were drilled, endlessly, in classical forms, which, of course, once had natural, organic bases. Until well into the twentieth century architects were taught the old rules of proportion, balance, and symmetry as well as the classical orders.

> For the first two hundred years or so, American architects and builders were guided by a fairly effective body of theoretical postulates, however unsophisticated or unformulated they may have often been. These principles derived in about equal parts . . . from folk experience and formal scholarly knowledge. . . . At any time prior to the death of Thomas Jefferson in 1826, both the architect and his building would have been disciplined, structured, 'held in shape,' by a clear and comprehensible reference frame of needs and means.

> Crisis in architectural esthetics did not appear till around the last century. Because of industrialization specialized designers sprang up. The architect then worked for the wealthy businessman, entrepreneur—gave him what he wanted but began to lose touch with the common man, factory worker, his needs. And the result of the architect's isolation from his real client is the increasing prevalence of the abstract, the formal, and the platitudinous in architectural and urban design.

> . . . the fundamental tensions (between the formal and the functional) remained; in fact, they grew steadily sharper with the rise of industrialism, and they are accurately reflected in the curriculums of our schools today. The effort of the schools to resolve this contradiction has been, generally speaking, to move toward increased emphasis on the academic, always at the expense of the craft elements of the field. From one point of view this has been both inevitable and desirable. Modern architectural problems can

Go ahead and say it. You think it's boring. Boring to have to learn about the Btu's of Trombe walls, the R-factors of earth berms or the efficiency of evacuated tube vs. flat plate collectors. Boring to be told to start designing buildings or planning urban developments with yet a whole new set of constraints. And not exhilarating to have to worry about creating new forms in response to new methods of heating, ventilating, and air conditioning.

Beauty, you assure us, will evolve naturally from energy-conscious design. Ethics, i.e.—solving the problem with an energy-conserving solution—carries its own aesthetic. Both types of extremists in this argument could be doomed to repeat history: one group, purely formal in orientation, losing a recently strengthened position to those who seek to respond to outside stimuli such as energy needs. The other who regards formal aspects of architecture as at best superfluous, at worst frivolous, may take too much for granted about architecture's public appeal. As shown by Modern Architecture's example, beauty does not always grow out of functional and technical solutions; it has proved to be more elusive.

A schism between energy-conscious architects and form-conscious ones could widen. Granted, it eventually may prove to be part of a dialectic that resolves itself in the synthesis of a new architecture. Right now the bifurcation of efforts results in a lot of awkward energy-saving buildings dotting the landscape, and a lot of well-designed buildings performing inefficiently and uneconomically.
SUZANNE STEPHENS

The cumulative objective effect of Ruskin's work was disastrous.
JAMES MARSTON FITCH

Architecture concerns itself only with those characters of any edifice which are above and beyond its common use.
JOHN RUSKIN

no more be solved by carpentry than can spacecraft be built by village black-smiths. However, the shift in training away from craftsmanship has been more toward mere technology than a truly scientific investigation of architecture as a whole . . . less and less able to encompass the complexity of modern technology, the architect's function is truncated. His designing becomes more and more a process of assemblage, more removed from functional necessity and therefore more susceptible to the pressures of fad and fashion.[1]

Classical study must have been maddening to the creative few, but to all the rest, the great majority, it must have been a comfort to be still learning the old rules while the world was changing. But classical principles could no longer be applied when the modern movement expanded. There were no precedents, no classical forms, no long history of what worked and what didn't, and there were all those new materials and mechanical systems to accommodate, so the teachers of architects had to develop ad hoc rules, rootless theories of proportion and scale, of composition and form, with you-know-what-kind of results. Students of architecture today are often pushed toward a deliberate unrelatedness to the earth, to an instability, toward making materials perform against their better natures in spite of a desperate need to get back onto better terms with our own planet.

Where the formal education of architects is concerned, their entire curriculum should be infused with a truly scientific (as opposed to a merely technical) approach to environmental and ecological problems.

JAMES MARSTON FITCH

The trouble is that mediocre design is teachable: it can be reduced to a system of rules. Good design can't. Frank Lloyd Wright, who at his best produced hundreds of poetically beautiful buildings, is virtually ignored by schools of architecture in this country. His eye and hand were so sure that in some of his buildings it's impossible to tell where the land influence ended and the man influence began. The title "organic" which he gave his work was not bestowed lightly. He knew what he was doing.

Wright never went to an architectural school. He studied engineering. And yet such was his artistic gift that his works were far more than the mere assembling of mechanical parts.

But how in the world do you produce the Wrights-to-be? There is no way. The man's architecture simply can't be packaged and labeled. Nothing is worse, either, than half-baked versions of Wrightian buildings. Perhaps they should never be attempted, and the schools of architecture are probably right in refusing to encourage anything that's too obviously rehashed Taliesin.

We're in a period of great change, and it's hard to see, from inside that period, what will be quite obvious to those who manage to outlive it. Certainly there are rules we must follow. There are life values to express.

[1]James Marston Fitch, *American Building 2: The Environmental Forces That Shape It,* Houghton Mifflin, Boston, 1975.

There are codes and site restrictions and historic precedent to guide us, and we know that simplicity, unity of theme, and design restraint will never let us down. We even have a few stunning examples of the new architecture to inspire us. But the design spark—the divine spark—continues to move in mysterious ways.

> The architect works with form and mass just as the sculptor does, and like the painter he works with color. But alone of the three, his is a functional art. It solves practical problems. It creates tools or implements for human beings and utility plays a decisive role in judging it.[2]

The Average Architect

The work of America's best-known architects is seen with some frequency in the pages of popular magazines and newspapers. We're all to some degree conscious of what it is the stars of the profession are doing. But what about the average U.S. architect, in Memphis, say, or Tacoma? Is he responding at all to the horrors of our increasingly poisonous environment?

It's hard to say. His current response, as measured by what we see of his architectural efforts along the street, is sometimes enough to ruin your day. But awareness has come late to our profession, and the new buildings being thrown up now are, after all, the products of design processes that went on two, three, or even four years ago. You have to visit a drafting room to see what's being designed today. There, overdue changes are beginning to appear. Nothing is focused yet however, and you see a lot of tokenism—solar panels, special glazings, those sort of things. You hear a lot of energy talk, too, much of it straight out of the environmental information in the ads the architects are reading. A lot of familiar old products are now being palmed off as being energy-saving, or good for the land, when it's pretty obvious they are nothing of the kind. It wouldn't matter if we weren't chewing up the countryside.

When my son Sam saw this drawing, the directness of his response surprised me. "All you have to do is run it backwards." Of course! It's just like the bombs in *Slaughterhouse Five* that rose out of inward-shrinking explosions that made buildings whole again, up into the bomb bays of airplanes that flew backward to their bases, where the bombs were removed, disassembled, reduced to their raw materials, put back into the earth, and covered with beautiful forests. Maybe such ideas are only pleasant dreams—fantasies of a world that could never be. Given our present state of laziness, that's all they seem. If anything is to change for

²S. E. Rasmussen, *Experiencing Architecture,* M.I.T. Press, Cambridge, Mass., 1959.

the better, however, we've got to produce a society that *can* run it all backwards, making rich, green cities out of urban deserts.

Architects have got to be among the leaders of that turnaround. It's not that we deserve such leadership. There just doesn't happen to be another group, ready with its T-squares and drawing boards, in sight.

The Stars of the Profession

In 1978, architect Philip Johnson made headlines when he suddenly forsook the slick steel and glass boxes he had helped make popular in America. According to his partner, John Burgee,

> We started to get into this direction because of the restrictions on the use of glass boxes brought on by the energy crisis—it seemed wrong to us to continue to do the International Style here. . . . We wanted to express this different time more fully, to try to get away from that flat surface and into carved and molded ones. . . . We are searching; we are looking for a way into the language of stone.[3]

Architect Robert Geddes sees architecture's possibilities in "the proper connections between social form and physical form" and believes that "an understanding of the nature of social institutions, their values, their norms of behavior, their rituals, is the most helpful way for an architect to get started."[4]

Nathan Silver, writing about the Corbusier revival in America and the five architects best known for its popularity—Peter Eisenman, Michael Graves, Charles Gwathmey, John Hejduk, and Richard Meier—sees their work as "temporary, minor, local and harmless; the product of mildly talented men," and defends their right to do such work in this way:

> If people want maintenance problems and high heating bills in their houses, there is as yet no law against that in America, and criticism of the ethics of a life conspicuously consumed in the privacy of one's home would surely be unlibertarian—what else could 'the pursuit of happiness' mean?[5]

He rightly sees the buildings themselves as no problem. Their problems will be corrected by later occupants or by the natural forces already at work upon them.

Here we see some of the most talented and influential architects in America apparently unaware of, or at least unmoved by, the biological foundations of all life and art. Here is Philip Johnson, the great taste-

Architecture that counts requires more than a good eye and a clever taste. Even the architect who indulges in tour de force *or private gesture must do so in the service of a larger framework of form, use, and technique that derives its meaning from a serious consideration of human and cultural factors and functional needs. An "appearance" architecture, which denies the factors that make building a complex social esthetic, is an architecture that lacks depth, vigor, and sublimity. It is fashion, not art.*

ADA LOUISE HUXTABLE

[3]*The New York Times,* May, 1978.
[4]*Architectural Record,* November 1977.
[5]Nathan Silver, "The House That Modernism Bulit," *Harper's,* August, 1977, p. 77.

maker of modern architecture, the AIA gold medalist, suddenly doing what some critics call "Chippendale skyscrapers" and rooftop falseworks while he searches for "the language of stone." Here is Geddes prescribing a comprehension of social form as the first step for an architect, and here are the Big Five, their misplaced Corbusian adventures admittedly too insignificant to have any physical effect on the world, but their every move monitored and admired by America's most sophisticated architects. And here is the vast army of American architects—all the professionals, all the students, and all the teachers—quietly trying to reproduce the stuff they see in the architectural press.

If ever we needed great designers, it is now. The environmental architecture of America is almost without exception depressingly ugly. Many people on first sight rightly decide they want no part of it. The great tastemakers and designers of our time flounder through stylistic revivals while the potential for really appropriate architecture goes unrecognized. This is perhaps the first time, in the hundred years since we began our stampede away from being an agrarian society, that we've had knowledge of, and at least some concern about, the physical and ecological consequences of architecture. We have a chance to turn the whole built environment—houses, buildings, highways, cities—off its suicidal course, and the brightest, most respected architects of our time refuse to have anything to do with it.

Ah, if only Frank Lloyd Wright were alive! Too bad he wasn't born 20 or 40 or even 60 years later. It's hard to believe he was brought into the world just after the Civil War, that he was a grown man before McKinley was president. Wright's buildings are still so stunningly modern they seem to be waiting in the future, somehow, for us to catch up with them. Wright, who lived his long life in an age when the world's supply of low-cost fuel and natural resources seemed endless, nevertheless experimented with passive solar heating, earth cover, berming, and task lighting. Just think what he might have given us if he'd been alive today!

The Larger View

In the largest sense, of course, it doesn't matter at all. The great issues of our time go far beyond architecture. Listen to what Lewis Mumford had to say on that subject when he was asked why he no longer writes about architecture:

> Because the real problems of civilization aren't soluble by the architect or by any one group of people. The real problems are much more profound and will require much more thorough study. That's why my work during the last 15 years has turned away from the specific problems of building and of

architectural form. I interpret what's been done and see the danger of the sterile life as an acceptable mode of living, but our problems are the problems of controlling nuclear energy, the problems of lessening the amount of industrial pollution, the problems of making the environment itself relatively stable and self-renewing and favorable to life of every kind, not just to man's life. We have to look after the bacteria and the insects as well as man if we're to have a really balanced environment. This is the profound meaning of the whole ecological process which is now gradually seeping into people.[6]

Seen in that light, architecture is, of course, nothing more than the thinnest of cosmetics.

Gentle Architecture

I've been having second thoughts about "watersaving" shower heads. Do they save more water than conventional spray nozzles? They seem certain only to save more than a fool. A waster with a gadget is still a waster; a shower taken by a saver is efficient regardless of nozzle type. The only water-saving shower head worth having is the one between the ears. That's where all real savings begin.

Architecture used to have boundaries. It started at the front wall and ended at the rear. A building was conceived, planned, financed, built, and occupied by a succession of specialists each of whom stuck to his appointed role. How the building affected, or was affected by, the condition of timberland in Oregon, or wildlife a mile down its watershed, or by Middle Eastern politics, had no part in the decisions that produced it. Not until recently were we even asked to think about such things. Now, all of a sudden, we see that they may be at the very heart of architecture.

It's beginning to dawn on us that our responsibilities reach beyond drawings and specifications, beyond the immediacy of Project 326. No longer can we simply walk away from it on dedication day, without a backward glance, already thinking of Project 327.

The materials with which we build are torn from the earth in ways so brutal they stun the first-time visitor. A logging site, a cement mine, or a gravel pit, especially when stumbled upon in an area of great natural beauty, can shock and repel. But we no longer trust first impressions. After an hour's tour of the place, calluses form. A week's exposure brings indifference. And a lifetime's? Who can say? The architect picks materials from his brightly colored catalogs, and the Caterpillars roll. From mine to mill to shop, the beautiful and the natural lose more and more of their identity as immense amounts of energy turn them bright

[6]Reprinted from an interview in *Tract,* No. 22, a quarterly issue by the Gryphon Press of Lewes, Sussex, England.

and plastic. Assembled as "completed" buildings, they have barely begun their decades of waste.

Each day, huge tractor-trailers enter the city. Coal, oil, gas, water, paper, nuclear power, gasoline, chemicals, food—all head straight for buildings, there to be turned into wastes and carted away by trucks and pipes, and by the winds, lost forever. Is this part of what architecture is all about? Of course it is. Architecture is involved all the way.

In a better world, architects would not only launch their buildings, they'd train the crews to sail them. What good is R-40 insulation if doors are left open? Or underground architecture if you drain a marsh to get it? Backward and forward, out of the land and into the future, buildings move through time at a cost no one can count. It's more a matter of earth-in-tuneness, anyway, than of accounting, this gentler way of building toward which we grope.

Right now, fuel prices are showing us the way. House fuel, car fuel, stomach fuel—each new shortage nudges us closer to world vision. Given enough scarcity and enough time we might produce an architecture to succeed Rudofsky's* But the cost! And every minute lost sees 10 million water-saving shower heads left turned on too long.

Not until the day when the architect takes his client by the hand and talks to him about the real costs of construction will we be on our way. Not until the client walks in, having already counted these costs, will we be almost there.

But architecture must be more than just a balanced budget. It must, in every sense, be art as well. The appropriate almost always is.

*Bernard Rudofsky's *Architecture without Architects* (Doubleday, New York, 1969) and *The Prodigious Builders* (Harcourt, New York, 1979) are essential for all who would design or build.

CHAPTER FOUR

Design Tools

Appropriateness

Sandtiquity is the name of a how-to book on the subject of pyramids and other classical buildings you can build on the beach using nothing more than a straightedge and damp sand. I am one of its authors. The others: photographer Connie Simo and sculptor Kappy Wells, my daughter.[1]

I learned more about architectural design in doing the sand structures for that book than I'd learned in many of the years before my happy adventure on the beach.

Sand—what a forgiving medium with which to make mistakes! All the unstable structures collapse, and the ugly ones get swept away by the incoming tide. It's hard to create an inappropriate sand architecture. Bad

[1]Taplinger, New York, 1980.

FIG. 4.1 *Dam, by Kappy Wells, Nauset Beach, Mass., 1977. (Connie Simo)*

stuff just won't stand up. Unlike buildings made of steel or wood, or even masonry or concrete, sand structures can't be forced to commit unnatural acts by the use of fasteners, reinforcings, props, adhesives, or ties. Sand does only what it has in its nature to do. You cannot build tall vertical surfaces or span large spaces. You can't build inverted pyramids or thin walls. Whatever stands up can be pretty safely used as an example of sand appropriateness.

Too bad we can't see the appropriateness of other materials that easily. Surely it's not good for us, architects or laypersons, to live with the inappropriate, unstable, inhumane, wasteful, and lifeless boxes of the new American downtown, or the garish, cheap, ill-proportioned junk along the Strip; yet the stuff continues to get built because the architects — *registered graduate architects* — who designed it know no better. They were never told about the embarrassment building materials experience when they are used without sensitivity or skill, so the circles of ugliness widen.

The theme of this book is environmental appropriateness in architecture, and in that light the idea of *building-material* appropriateness, of proper proportion and use, may seem at first a bit trivial or off the track until it becomes apparent that the overall question, which is life and our response to it, has appropriateness at its core. I am sure we'll never succeed in taming ourselves unless both our inner and our outer uglinesses get corrected together.

A Sense of Turning

How tempting it is to build pyramids and other simple sand structures on these Cape Cod beaches! I can hardly resist the temptation to drop to my knees and build a temple whenever I am there, winter or summer. The best part is the utter simplicity of it all: Make a sand pile, pack it a bit, and cut. Slice, scrape, slice, and behold! an ancient monument stands upon the timeless strand. That's the joy of it. The fun is in the refinements, in the straightening and sharpening of the corners and the edges, in the pressing smooth of the surfaces, and in the adding of convincing little details. The surprise is in the sense of planet it evokes.

I work for what seem like only minutes, and suddenly an hour has passed, then two. I have so much fun, time seems to race by, the sun's shadows on the sandworks changing so rapidly I suddenly have a sense of movement, of turning with the spinning earth, below the endless sun. Maybe most people have that kind of planet-consciousness all the time. I don't. On ordinary days, if I notice the changing sun positions at all, I notice them in an east-to-west, morning-to-night kind of way, unaware that it is the earth carrying me eastward that makes the sun appear to move west.

The microregional energy forces of sun, air, earth, water, and living organisms as the ingredients of an energy-responsive architecture will give it a microregional character. As underground architecture or an increase of on-site or local materials is used to converse energy, the regional image of architecture will be reinforced.

RICHARD CROWTHER

I can't begin to prove it, but I know that the more conscious we become of ourselves as riders on a lonely planet, the more quickly we'll move toward living sanely together.

A Touch of Outrage

The environment that concerns me most at the moment, of course, is the one I'm in. It's not necessary that I give you its address. Take my word for the fact that it's pretty bad. It just happens to be the place where I must be today. I am engulfed in vinyl ceiling tiles surfaced with vinyl sheets, wallpaper done in nonfading vinyl colors, and resilient floor tile made of—you guessed it—vinyl (actually vinyl *asbestos,* which makes it even worse). The countertop nearby is covered with plastic laminates; the paint on the door, the trim, and all the cabinets in the room are some kind of plastic product. My imagination is probably doing me more damage at this moment than the vinyl is, but I can't help feeling caged in this plastic chemical atmosphere, knowing as I do that repeated exposure to it not only kills the soul, it may do a pretty good job on the body as well. If the people who must work in the factories that produce this junk are having physical problems because of it, surely some of those consequences are going to rub off, over the years, on those of us who use it where we live and work.

Many people are concerned about pollution. Many people are concerned about nuclear power. Others are concerned about other things, but few of us leap into action until we are touched directly. That's why the *immediate* environment is so important. We need it as a stimulant. Number one is a lot more important to each of us than is the guy next door.

Oh, if only we didn't adapt to such environments so quickly! If only we could sustain the sense of outrage we feel on first coming into contact with these phony chemical surfaces! But already I can feel a tide of complacency moving in. My stay here is only temporary, and soon I'll think of other things, other problems. But what about the permanent occupants of this space? What will happen to them? What will happen to all the hundreds of millions who are forced to spend their lives wrapped in plastic, so far from that silent green world in which they evolved?

I don't know.

Neighborliness

I do know that people are tremendously interested in architectural alternatives; there's no longer the kind of resistance to them there once was. The word "underground" still tends to chill a lot of people, but when they see that it means something sunny and dry instead of dark and damp the chill quickly gives way to curiosity and acceptance. Actually, the whole point of an underground, or even a gentle, architecture is that of being a better neighbor. We're all bad neighbors now: all of us dumping on each other. Think of the rainwater runoff, the smoke, the noise, and the light that spills from our own onto our neighbors' properties. Is that any way to get along?

It seems quite clear to me that when we adopt wilderness criteria of the kind outlined on the 15-point graph (Chapter 2) as our design guides we can throw out all zoning laws and build, *without offense to anyone,* almost any kind of building without the disastrous environmental consequences that all architecture produces today. Zoning, as we know it, is at best stifling in its pigeonholing of all human activities, and at worst racist in its effects. I'm no more interested than anyone else in having a gas station or a steel mill next door to my house—not if they're built under today's kinds of rules. But when we've learned to build properly we can welcome such neighbors.

With nondegradation standards for all land, we could allow *anything* to be built anywhere. Then we'd have a diversified society again, a healthy society and healthy land. Children would again be able to get most of their education in the right way, directly from the wonderfully diverse and exciting world all around them. Under today's compartment-type zoning most kids grow up bored in boring residential communities, exposed only to other bored kids and other families very much like the ones they see at home. We can have rich diversity and a clean environment as well if we care enough to be good neighbors.

Smaller Spaces

Science fiction illustrators have often produced visions so stunning I've forgotten to look behind their glittering surfaces. Recently I saw one which depicted a floating city in the sky. It was the world dream we all pray for—sparkling skies, unspoiled nature, and glorious engines bathed in light. Sweet harmony: no strikes, no garbage dumps, no used car lots, no terrorists, no wars, no hurricanes, no disasters. But you won't get me to ride in one of those sky towns until I've bought a little more life insurance. The pursuit of another dream seems far more promising. It may mean chapped hands and runny noses, sweat stains and poison ivy, and flopping into bed utterly tired now and then, but the rewards are tremendous. When engine noises fade, inner voices are heard, and the fabulous cities in the sky turn into carnival prizes, things to suspend, along with the baby's first pair of shoes, from the car mirror—tinselled, misleading refusals to face our own animality. Compared to the wonders of even the humblest weed, Sky City is a Rube Goldberg contraption clunking along up there. If we were wiser, we'd stop being excited by such things and fall to our knees in gratitude for the far greater gift we were given—the seldom-used ability to appreciate this rich earth spectacle around us.

The science fiction of architecture, with rare exceptions, is hopelessly man-centered. Sky cities, sea cities, bubble cities, stack cities, instant cities, media cities; biotecture, agrotecture, videotecture, cybertecture—what a roster! One can imagine wildlife crying out in terror, "What in hell are those bastards going to do next? Try this, try that. Whatever happened to the facts of life? Doesn't the man-animal know about the budget?" For life does have a budget; its currency is air, water, land, and a day's ration of sunlight. If you think this year is extravagantly beyond its budget, imagine what the year 2000 will be like. And yet we architects keep offering man-centered solutions to all space-age challenges. Fun without substance. "Hey, this looks exciting," or "Why don't we try that? The magazines are sure to publish it." I know; I've succumbed to the same temptation all too often.

Just think how different an architect's work would be if he were forced to start a project by reciting its fundamentals in an elementary-school sort of way:

Here is an animal called a human being. What are its characteristics?

- It needs air, water, and food.
- It produces heat, breath, sweat, and other wastes.
- It needs insulation from temperature extremes.
- It needs protection against things like rain, wind, dust, insects, peeping Toms, and burglars.
- It was designed to live in a quiet environment.
- It craves mental stimulation.
- It needs love and approval from its fellow animals.
- It likes comfort.
- If its tendency to eat too much and avoid exercise is not discouraged, it dies too soon.
- The budget for its total sustenance cannot exceed the amount of air, water, food, and natural resources which can be taken from its proportionate share of planet surface without degrading the life-supporting qualities of that area.

That would send us back to our drawing boards, wouldn't it? All of a sudden, in place of lifeless domes and shining towers, in place of cyber-, cryo-, electro-, agro-, chemitecture, you'd begin to see shelter-pod structures and solar-pit houses, or better yet, you might even see us architects out there actually building earth structures with our own hands instead of forever selling our bubbled whims to the trusting clients.

In its landmark Mt. Laurel case, the New Jersey Supreme Court ruled that towns may no longer practice racial or economic discrimination through zoning—no more all-white suburbs with zoning requirements so exclusionary the poor are forever barred. The ruling is bound to have vast effects we can't foresee. It may even force us to face and solve our number one social disgrace, racism. But one of the still-unperceived side effects of the Mt. Laurel case is its other influence in architecture—the return of the tiny house. Obviously, we can't go on subsidizing ever-more-expensive low-income housing. Sooner or later we've got to start paying as we go by building only that which we can afford—small, in other words. Both the dollar budget and the life budget demand it.

Mt. Laurel may have opened the door to healthful housing practices, but the very idea of small houses is repulsive to most of us. We base our whole status system on house size, and nobody wants to be at the bottom of the scale, not until the fuel runs out, that is. But the millions of people who run away to the yacht clubs on summer weekends can't wait to squeeze into their tiny, floating quarters. That's because there's no stigma attached to using them. Far from it, in fact. America's boating fraternity proves there's plenty of appeal in small spaces. They're sometimes more appealing than large, impersonal ones. Besides, the best large spaces are out-of-doors, anyway. We can't begin to compete with nature when it comes to space drama. And look at the way restaurant booths get filled before the tables do.

When I must enter spaces that seem unsafe, or smell bad, or have no horizon outlet through which the human spirit can expand, I want to flee. A sense of spaciousness is, to a large degree, a matter of design.

Architects must learn to build life-budget houses. We've got to rebuild or restore to a natural condition all the constructed parts of this still-rich land before it's too late. It will take every skilled and unskilled hand, not just for a year but for a lifetime. World energy resources are being bled to death heating America's 70 million wasteful housing units. We've got to get back in step again by building houses and other buildings so efficient, and in many cases so small, they can be heated by the sun, or by various bioconversion processes, or, ideally, merely by body heat alone. But we're a long way from that. New housing units can be small enough that even in the densely populated new villages of the cities, there'll be room to let gardens surround, and even cover, each house. Then we won't see this kind of bureaucratic nonsense on wall posters anymore: "Let's clean up our air." Or "Let's clean up our waters." It isn't possible for us to clean up skies and rivers once they get dirty. They can do that only by themselves. Our job is to manage wastes and conserve resources. It doesn't involve skies and rivers at all. Once we do *our* part we'll find that the skies and the waters have somehow miraculously cleaned themselves. That's when we'll know we've been doing something right. And who knows? Maybe then one of those great sky cities will come floating by, out of the blue, as silent and as pure as the clouds.

But I'm not going to hold my breath until that happens.

Preparing the Client

I don't like to surprise my clients. As soon as we meet I let them know of my interests and concerns. I try before we get too far along to pave the way for the recommendations I know I'll be making. But, every once in a while, no matter how diplomatic my forewarnings have been, the client will feel, when I've made my proposals, that I have gone too far, and, as a result, my commission will be of very short duration. But that sort of thing happens to all architects. Statistically, most projects evaporate before they reach the construction stage anyhow.

Here's one that didn't.

I was asked, not long ago, to visit a rural environmental center to be interviewed for the job of designing its new facilities. When I arrived for my first meeting I found that a lot more than architecture was needed. The place looked less like my idea of an environmental center than a shopping center. There was too much paving, there were too many cars, too many lights burning, too much air conditioning. All the food prepared for the daily busloads of schoolchildren served by the center was of the highly processed, heat-and-serve type, and it was served in disposable containers! I was appalled, but, having been taught, long ago, how a guest is to behave, I kept my eyes open and my mouth shut. Later, back at my office, I prepared a lengthy commentary and sent it off to the center's administrator. Instead of sketches for a building addition, what she got was something which read, in part, like this:

> . . . I came away with so many impressions I hardly know where to begin.
>
> At the beginning, I suppose, and right up there at the top of the list, is a world environmental crisis so severe there's little chance of our pulling through it without first undergoing a disaster of such proportions I can't even bear to think about it. But *I* don't have to tell *you;* that's what you're there for—to tell the world about the life-miracle and its offer of a way out of our mess.
>
> That being the case, I think the first job of the Center is to *express* its commitment to that way. I'm talking about the visual, outward expression of an idea, of things I didn't see during my visit the other day. All I saw were cars and more cars, acres of asphalt, more acres of machine-mowed grass,

of eroding hillsides, and of buildings that were all-too-obviously heat leaking, sun wasting, rain shedding, power burning, and sewage dumping.

Am I criticizing *you?* Of course not. I wouldn't have been invited to visit the Center if you'd been happy with the way things were. If I were your architect I'd want to be sure, first of all, that *every* aspect of life at the Center was aimed at making us well again. I can't find a dividing line between architecture and the use of aerosol sprays, or poisons, or paper plates, or conventional sewage disposal. It's all part of the same thing, which is human life on earth, and I'd push strongly for bans on all life-degrading practices in order that harmony and not discord be both the apparent and the actual theme of the Center.

You will have thrown your building funds away if, after they've been spent, people of all ages don't come away dazzled from having been given a glimpse of the might-have-been, of a world so appropriate and beautiful, and so unlike your nearest town today, as to be almost unbelievable.

Every creature except man builds unobtrusive or hidden buildings. Every creature except man has solar energy as its sole energy source. Every creature except man recycles all its wastes, not just some of them. What a difference from the things we see at the Center today! Imagine having to burn electric lights in the daytime! Imagine having to air-condition! Imagine having to heat a building artificially! Imagine dropping human wastes into drinking water! Imagine having buildings that stand *on* a site, on the site of an *environmental* center, like so many suburban ranch houses!

If you're ever going to make a measurable impact on The Mess, you're going to have to stun us. These are desperate times.

Tear up the paving, tear down the buildings, demolish the toilets, grow your own food, discard the lawn mowers, use the sun, use the wind, use the earth—not all at once, of course, but as soon as possible. Five years, ten years, it doesn't matter, but *set the goal right now,* and then get started.

Imagine stepping inside a wooded hill and finding bright, dry, sun-filled rooms there! Imagine finding windows shining in flowered hillsides! Imagine seeing the kids themselves at work, making and laying the porous paving blocks, planting the new rooftops, growing the food. Talk about environmental education! The Center would be its own best teacher.

I'm sorry to run on this way, but it's late and there's a lot to be done if we are to have a prayer of surviving . . ..

The owners were full of enthusiasm. "Let's get on with it" was their immediate response to my letter.

I've found that most people are far more concerned and far more willing to make changes than I'd imagined, and there's nothing so conducive to good work as having that kind of support.

Psychology

"But are there psychological ramifications to gentle architecture?" people ask. Of course there are. There are psychological ramifications to everything. But don't waste your time on them. Of course there are prejudices, of course there are misconceptions, and of course there are people who are afraid of earth-sheltered living, if they've never seen what it's like. And, of course, there are already many grant-funded studies under way to see what the effects of those prejudices and misconceptions are going to be. But they're all irrelevant froth.

All who see it know that this kind of architecture is appealing, sunny, soothing, and secure—more like the environment from which the human species evolved than is anything else we have today. If a few people are prejudiced, let them be. Their prejudgments will soon be wiped away by direct evidence and need not be catered to by yet another round of psychological coddling.

It's the architects who should be studying.

Keeping Up

If you want to see an architect jump, walk up behind one and say "recertification." That dread word means trouble, and he doesn't want to hear about it. He's got enough on his mind without having to worry about taking his exams all over again. At the moment, we architects are licensed—registered—for life. Once we pass our exams, all we have to do to stay registered is pay a yearly registration fee and stay out of serious trouble.

But a new idea is emerging: recertification on some regular basis. It's a thought that terrifies us because most of us just barely made it the first time. We had to pass 4 days of tough written examinations before we could call ourselves registered architects and hang out our shingles. Now the thought of going through it all again, of having to ask our hardened old brains to relearn long-forgotten things like the date of the Parthenon, or to solve complex structural equations, shakes us to our very foundations.

I don't know any details yet of the proposed recertification procedure, but I'm sure that when they finally appear we'll see that weeks, if not months, of advance warning will be given us and that the exams will be only watered-down versions of the originals, arranged just to satisfy the letter of the law. In other words, tokenism. One thing I do know: the exams never will be sprung on us by surprise. Our organization has too much political clout to allow that. But what if we *were* given spot checks, instant exams without warning? What if we had to meet at any moment the standards we expect of brand new architects? I doubt that 5 percent of us would keep our licenses.

Sure, we older architects have years of valuable experience under our belts; sure, we've had to learn about a real-life architecture the schools never taught us. Still, what about all those new techniques, all the new priorities in architecture, all the things that came along after we left school? What about low-impact technology, biological imperatives, energy costs, high-rise catastrophe, solar heating, automated housing, and the computerization of a hundred new disciplines? "Huh? What's that all mean?" we say as we rush blindly into a future we can barely recognize. The fact is that most of us are simply not qualified to practice the very profession in which we now make our living.

"Well, so what?" you can say, "Maybe we don't produce the best of all possible architectures. That's not the end of the world. Look at all the trashy-looking new buildings out there along the highway. Admittedly, they were designed by registered professional architects. And, admittedly, they may be almost soul-crushing in their ugliness, but they're hardly what you'd call a threat to life safety."

I'll accept that argument for the moment, but I dare you to apply the same reasoning to the work of the medical profession. My own doctor is an intelligent person, but I doubt that a surprise medical exam would find her much better prepared than a surprise architectural exam would find me. Why not just leave well enough alone? She does her job pretty well; I do mine. She's managed to keep me in reasonably good health, and none of my buildings have collapsed.

But is that all we want, just to get by? Isn't that exactly the kind of standard that's caused so much of today's mess? We've produced a whole civilization based on mediocrity, on throwaway automobiles, on honky-tonk highway business, and on nonrenewable resources. If someone doesn't stop us, we'll go right on producing it.

Tougher standards won't ruin us, they'll be good for us. Only higher, tougher standards can make us search for a gentler and better architecture.

I took a recertification exam recently. It was a voluntary one, carrying no threat to my registration. It was one of several sample exams being evaluated by the National Council of Architectural Registration Boards for possible use in the recertification programs which may come along in the next few years.

I passed it, barely. The answers were of the multiple-choice type, and in many cases I didn't think *any* of the answers were right. Most of mine were guesses, not based on what I believe about the state of architecture and construction but on what I felt were the desired responses. Many of the questions involved such things as converting Btus to kilowatts, and knowing the various R-factors for insulations, none of which I've ever been able to keep in my head. I know better, now, than even to try; I rely on the experts in those fields. The exercise did little more than teach me that recertification is a lot more complicated a subject than I thought it was. Not only are there no absolutely right answers to anything, but the choice of subjects in which an architect should be most competent is nowhere near having been made. Maybe architects aren't even the ones to make that decision. In any case, it will be years before a workable system emerges. But it's coming. And if it's based on life values the good it can do will be incalculable.

Using the Earth

Right now the gentle architecture movement is divided into splinters: solarizers, undergrounders, conservers. I can think, for instance, of only fifteen or twenty architects now regularly practicing, let alone specializing in, underground architecture, but I also know of well over 20,000 people in the market for underground buildings. Our sluggish profession is once again being drawn into better ways by those who read *Popular Science* or who want something a little more challenging out of life than a rubber-stamp house and a couple of big cars.

People should realize that you really don't need to segregate us as "gentle" or "brutal" architects. The techniques of using sunlight and earth shelter are not all that mysterious or complicated. Physical laws apply with equal force no matter where or how you build. Gentle architecture is so close to becoming an accepted part of the mainstream it won't be "exceptional" much longer. Soon, if not right now, a person will be able to go to any architect, anywhere, demand better architecture, and get it. It might even turn out to be fairly well done, for there's nothing like a tough challenge to get the old creative juices flowing, especially if there's the promise of a little fun in the venture as well.

Underground architecture, a subspecies of gentle architecture, is already in wide practice, and it has the facilities of an impressive organization available for any help needed in developing earth-architecture skills.

The American Underground Space Association is a nonprofit group open to all persons interested in the use of underground space. One of its major aims is to encourage the exchange of information about all aspects of the subject. The association produces a bimonthly journal called *Underground Space.* AUSA also publishes an impressive book called *Earth Sheltered Housing Design.* It's a big, 8½- by 11-in, 310-page paperback crammed full of design and energy information, structural and waterproofing facts, building code reviews, financial tips, illustrative designs, descriptions of underground houses, and appendixes packed with tables, graphs, and information sources.*

*For information write to the American Underground Space Association, Department of Civil and Mineral Engineering, University of Minnesota, Minneapolis, MN 55455.

Over 25,000 persons have written to me about their interest in underground architecture, and I am logging their addresses in the AUSA computer, hoping that over the years I'll be able to check, now and then, on how the pioneers of this booming offshoot of mainstream architecture helped it grow to a more respectable size.

Mining is also one of AUSA's interests. Its parent department's "Mineral Engineering" title seems to be tinged with the land-expolitation attitude that has caused so much of the world's distress. That bothers me a little, and I've had more than a few discussions with my AUSA friends over that side of their activities. Those in favor assure me that new mining and land restoration techniques (and the new laws that generated them) mean much less land destruction. But all the mining—both strip mining and deep mining—that I've ever seen has been just plain appalling to me. It leaves behind it bitter unemployment, acid rivers, and barren land.

Many of the mineral engineering people, of course, see all talk of reduced dependence on the extraction of resources as impossibly naive. They say there's no other way, that we must have those resources no matter what course society takes.

Like everything else, I suppose, the American Underground Space Association is a mixture of the forces of evil and the forces to which I belong, those of goodness and enlightenment. If you want to talk about dichotomy, look at the U.S. Department of Energy. Overpoweringly nuclear-, coal- and oil-oriented, it nevertheless has its solar-energy enthusiasts. They're convinced, as I am, that if we manage to avoid a final irradiation of one sort or another, the solar view is bound to prevail, perhaps within our lifetimes. Compared to the struggle the solar people are having, the differences among the AUSA factions seem far more manageable, and the mineral engineers out there at the University of Minnesota seem so bright I'm willing to concede that what you might call gentle mining is a real possibility after all.

Books

Between the resources of organizations like the American Underground Space Association and those available in most libraries, a wide range of soft-tech information is available to everyone. Some of the books that have impressed me most are the following.

■ One is *Architecture Without Architects: A Short Introduction to Non-Pedigreed Architecture (Doubleday, New York, 1969)* by Bernard Rudofsky. It was published in the mid-sixties by the Museum of Modern Art, and it's on its way to becoming a classic. I think it's the most important book you could possibly read on the subject of building design and on how to respond to the environment. It's simply a collection of photographs of buildings built all over the world, by people who had no architectural training at all. It's full of beautiful, beautiful, buildings that put to shame most architecture done *with* architects.

- Another book of Rudofsky's, almost a sequel to *Architecture Without Architects,* is *The Prodigious Builders.* It carries the first book's theme to greater heights. Important reading for anyone who cares about architectural design.

- Also important is *Solar-Heated Buildings of North America,* by William Shurcliff. A Harvard physicist, Dr. Shurcliff is *the* chief authority in the field. He knows how things work. His survey of existing solar-heated buildings looks behind the window dressing that architects generate, taking you to the heart of each project—how it works, why it may not work, how it could be improved.

- Bruce Anderson's *The Solar Home Book,* is probably the best seller among solar publications. Written by an MIT architecture graduate who started with a one-man energy business in the early seventies, and who now finds himself the head of a booming little consulting and publishing empire, it's packed with basic solar principles, details, data, and examples.

- *Soft Tech,* published by *The Co-Evolution Quarterly,* covers most aspects of what some of us call alternative technology. It gets right down to the nuts and bolts of the matter, with pictures, sources, and good, responsible writing.

- Any of the illustrated books on the work of Frank Lloyd Wright. Leaf through the pages and let the work of America's native genius soak in. Wright was a once-in-a-millenium architect; his buildings come as close to being earth music as anything imaginable. A master artist, his work grew directly out of nature's examples.

- *Earth Sheltered Housing Design* is another good one. It was discussed earlier in this chapter.

- *The Co-Evolution Quarterly.* A publication that deals with almost everything, mainly offering alternatives to the world we've created for ourselves, but not limiting itself to that. *CQ* is full of art, cartoons, photos, stories, how-to articles, sources, reviews—everything that might be of interest to a reader who wants something free of the commercial values usually found in advertiser-supported publications.

- The name John Holt is well known among educators and millions of parents as well. His many books on the subject of education show him moving further and further away from the whole idea of schooling. Now he believes there should be none, that children would best grow into this world if they learned life by living it, if they absorbed information, skills, and knowledge the way children always did before schools were invented. He publishes a newsletter called *Growing Without School* that is good reading whether or not you have children, or whether or not you're interested in education. It doesn't take much exposure to John Holt to see how schooling converts the open, wide-ranging mind of a child into the narrow, unthinking, rubber-stamp mind of an adult. (Growing Without School, 308 Boylston St., Boston, MA 02116.)

▪ The New Alchemy Institute at Woods Hole, Massachusetts, is operated by an impressive group of young scientists, technicians, gardeners, and writers whose work in aquaculture, farming, wind power, composting, solar heating, earth shelter, and related fields is most impressive. They publish a beautiful journal each year in which they mix dreams and facts to produce pictures of the bright world we're entering. (New Alchemy Institute, Box 47, Woods Hole, MA 02543)

Being an easterner, I'm bound to miss good work and good books from other places, but rather than try to comment on things about which I know too little I'll end my resources list here, with the following commercial message: the books I've written are all listed in the bibliography.

Codes

The acceptance of gentle architecture is growing, even in the building departments of towns and cities. Here in Brewster, Massachusetts, for instance, the building inspector is highly enthusiastic about the idea because he sees its potential for solving some of the problems caused by conventional construction on Cape Cod.

But then, I've never had much trouble with building codes. When I have, *I've* usually been the one who was wrong. Just like the body of civil and criminal law that was developed in this country, building codes have come about in response to need. Every time I read that a 2-hour-rated fire enclosure must surround all public stairways, I am reminded of all the stair disasters which had to occur before that stair-safety code could be written.

As a species we have an almost criminal record of land destruction on this continent, and I feel at times as if the best solution to the environmental mess would be some kind of catastrophe great enough to eliminate all human life. But in my saner moments I know there is catastrophe enough already. If gentle architecture is to take root, it must, before all other considerations, be safe. Safety is *the* architectural priority. Life safety must come before all other considerations: before shelter, before environment, before energy, before esthetics. Generally this goes without saying, and most architects head straight for the building-code books when they begin their research into the requirements for an unfamiliar building type. But among the architects of the alternative technology movement one often sees a tendency to disparage codes as being obstructive to all progress. If, for instance, the local code won't allow the use of plastic pipes where cast iron and copper were by tradition the only choices, maybe it isn't because of a conspiracy between the politicians and the metal pipe people, or between the politicians and the labor unions. Maybe there are good reasons to go slowly on such things. I'm no chemist, but I'm not eager to drink a lifetime's ration of water that's been slowly eroding the walls of a polyvinylchloride pipe—not after what I've read about such substances. Somehow I feel more comfortable with erosion particles from iron or copper pipes. I've seen iron pills in the health food store but never any polyvinylchloride ones.

And look at the way other building materials have let us down. Lead-based paints and asbestos products come immediately to mind. In many states laws now require that leaded paints and asbestos ceilings be removed from thousands of buildings. (Where all that debris will get dumped and what the effect of the dumping will be on future generations seem not to have been too well thought out. This should give us further pause before we adopt new materials where the old ones have had good records.) If the prices of iron and copper pipes seem too high, the appropriate response is not to switch immediately to plastic but to use less of both the iron and copper: to simplify, to change oneself rather than the piping.

In the last few years, I have received thousands of letters from people all over the country asking my advice about such things as underground architecture and solar heating. I hear from architects and nonarchitects alike, and I am appalled at the number of potentially unsafe buildings expressed by the designs they send me. First, by far, in this regard are hillside, earth-covered houses in which the occupants could be trapped in the event of a fire. It's true that many underground buildings are inherently fireproof, but it's also true that their contents are not. A roomful of furniture may not generate a lot of heat, but smoke and panic often kill as effectively as flames. I spend a lot of time warning people of the hazards they're creating.

One of the most common is the windowless bedroom. I see it on plans in which the daytime spaces face the southern glass wall and the nighttime ones lurk in lightless gloom, deep inside the hill. Often there's only one way out of those back areas, and if that way is blocked by fire, smoke, furniture, or fallen structural members—goodbye family! Another lethal possibility is the skylighted atrium house in which not only is there just one way out (often by way of an unsafe stair), but also the horrifying prospect of one's being basted alive, while attempting to use that one exit, as melted plastic drops from the burning dome.

That's why I'm so much in favor of building codes. We have such a bad record in everything else we do; we're really lucky to have this means of keeping ourselves more or less on the track.

Costs

If building costs limit gentle architecture's use to high-income people, it will never have any value. All you have to do is fly over an American city to grasp the dimensions of the housing problem, or visit an unemployment office or welfare agency to be reminded of the money squeeze that's so unending a way of life to so many. To most of us, architecture and new construction, let alone this special thing called gentle architecture, are in another world; and to say, for instance, that earth-covered construction often costs less than conventional construction is not to say very much at all.

Still, a lot of middle- and low-income people *are* managing to build these buildings in spite of the cost barriers. The motive behind the work must be a lot more powerful than anything generated by high fuel prices alone. There seems to be an earth-consciousness brewing, one that may well overturn this whole vinyl-coated, food-additive, cancerous society. Solid permanence, shelter, and freedom from high fuel bills are big parts of the movement, but it's based on a wider foundation, something no one has quite identified yet, and a surprising number of people are taking the plunge, building houses and other small buildings themselves, sometimes with the help of architects, but more often without.

What bothers me most about the whole building-costs situation is the fact that the individual banker has replaced the individual conscience. If he says you can't afford to build responsibly he is offering a fiscal answer to a moral question. If conventional architecture is morally wrong then it must not even be an option, and, by the tens and hundreds and thousands, people are beginning to make the silent commitment to less destructive ways, forcing the native American genius to stir again. That's where our hope for lower building costs lies.

CHAPTER FIVE

Land

If you'd like to see a bit of instant geology, come with me one day when it rains to the little valley beyond the new shopping center. Even before we get there you'll hear the roar made by tons of wild storm water charging down the pipe from the parking lots. It's truly a terrifying sound. The 26 acres of buildings and blacktop that make up that shopping center pour 600,000 gallons into the pipe every time an inch of rain falls.

Erosion

As frightening as the drain roar, though, is what the water does after it leaves the pipe. Layers of earth that had lain untouched for centuries are sliced away in seconds. Blasting into what was once a quiet little ravine, the linear tidal wave chews up blocks of earth that took ages to build and spews them downstream into lifeless sand flats wherever slack water occurs. Along with this flood go the oil drippings, the cigarette butts, and all the other by-products of our automotive society. Literally within minutes the entire valley form can change. Little cliffs of earth will appear and then collapse where a few minutes earlier tottering trees and vines still held the bank. And once the ground cover goes, the never-ending business of bank stabilization must begin. Sandbags may last for a while; concrete or steel sheet piling somewhat longer. But it's a losing battle, and from then on, the magic will have gone from the valley.

In the valley of the shadow of the supermarkets you need not wait a million years between shows. You can see it all in minutes: sandbars appear, disappear, and reappear, mimicking geologic actions that used to take generations, sometimes even millenia, at a time when nature had more of an even chance. It's like what the forty-niners did to California's untouched valleys, except that here you see it on a grander scale; America today may lose in a week as much as California's valleys lost in a decade.

Overpaving

Each year, we withdraw another 10 million acres from the green side of the national ledger. As those acres are turned into what we call improved land they become very efficiently paved, if not with blacktop or concrete or roofing materials, then paved with closely mowed turf—lawn grass— which is no slouch as a paving material, either. Neatly trimmed grass can be counted on to repel almost half as much rain water as a shingled roof. We've called ourselves the Affluent Society, the Effluent Society, and the Great Society, but I think of us simply as the Pavers. Never before has man or any other creature gone about the waterproofing of this planet with such a vengeance.

It's a deadly situation. Forgetting for a moment all the plants and wild-life denied existence on paved sites, forgetting the soul-crushing ugliness of vast paved areas, forgetting even the erosion they cause, *the amount of water denied access to the land by our black, white, and green paving exceeds the total water consumption of the United States!* It has to. It can't be calculated exactly, for no one has yet documented the total surface covered by our cities, towns, roads, houses, lawns, factories, airports, schools, railroad yards, refineries, warehouses, and shopping centers. But fourth-grade multiplication will prove the point.

Water Waste

The city of Philadelphia, in whose suburbs I lived until 1977, has an area of 135 square miles. Its annual rainfall is 45 inches. If you convert all those miles, inches, acres, and feet into gallons you get a staggering *122 billion* as Philadelphia's annual share of the nation's rainfall. And do you know how much water her thousands of homes and water-wasting factories consume each year? 125 billion gallons! Just the amount of rain that falls within the city limits. You might think, then, after reading all this, that Philadelphia has no water shortage. But there's a catch: Philadelphia hardly uses the water that's given her. No, most of those sweet, fresh raindrops are poured away, unused, into the city's two vile rivers. Then the city goes upstream to get its own supply. It drinks diluted sewage and throws its rainwater away!

But don't blame the Philadelphians. They do only what you and I and the people of Tokyo and Chicago are doing. We've all waterproofed ourselves so well that the rain just can't soak in. We've changed the very nature of entire continents. I wonder it anyone has ever made a study of American place-names in the light of this massive thwarting of nature. Has anyone lately thought about the Mesas that are no longer Verde, the Rios no longer quite so Grande, the thousands and thousands of pineless Pine Streets, the now-brown Greenvilles, and murky Clearwaters? Each of us is surrounded by a roster of vanished riches. Near my home in Cherry Hill (which, incidentally, has few cherry trees or hills) are Haddonfield, Collingswood, and Maple Shade, none of which could possibly be recognized by its descriptive name today. And I can't even bear to tell you about Fairview.

What an eye-opener it would be if we updated those names to the more appropriate Deadways, Shedwells, and Graymuds! The most appropriate and probably the most common new city name would have to be Runoff (which has a kind of cosmopolitan, Russian sound to it, now that I think about it—Runoff, U.S.A., my home town).

There's a lesson in this: if enough rain to accommodate its 2 million water-wasting people falls on the few square miles of Philadelphia, it follows that enough rain to accommodate all of America's 220 million other water-wasting people must fall on an area only 100 times as large, *or an area far less in size than that of Pennsylvania!* But that doesn't include the huge river-drinks taken by irrigation and industry. They use ten times as much as people do. Still, the runoff from lawns alone is staggering: they repel up to 50 *trillion* gallons each year. That's half the water budget for the entire country.

Impressive, wouldn't you say? It points up one of the reasons why most of us in the United States are in big water trouble: we throw the stuff away by building and landscaping as we do. On our roofs we could build watergates—devices for slowing the rush to the rainspouts—so the rain would have time to soak in when it reached the ground. We could even use giant sponges. But the best way by far is the natural way, doing what nature always did on the land: plant trees or shrubs or grasses in deep, cheap mulch. Such watergates have to be planned with care, of course, from the initial concept to the final cover-up, but they hold great promise. Watergate architecture, or underground architecture, or whatever kind of architecture you care to call it, makes good sense in a lot of ways, and it's been around for a long, long time.

Underground Architecture

I can picture the conventional caveman of the comic strip, the prototype Fred Flintstone, as he must have looked when he saw a cave for the first time in his life. It couldn't have been very many minutes later that the idea of underground architecture was born. That was perhaps a million years ago, long before modern man, as we know him, started inventing war and bigotry (and the religions to excuse them) and learning how to lay continents bare and to overbreed himself.

In the millenia between then and now he has also managed to invent or discover many kinds of shelter other than caves, but architecture— really great architecture—remains, as it began, an *earth* art: an expression, fashioned in the earth's own materials, of the particular culture in which the architect-as-human lives. And despite all the great advances in the techniques of building above ground, man has never completely abandoned underground construction. Fossils from every age and reports from every continent prove that this most ancient of architecture has always been in use.

Still, the idea of an underground architecture *for the purpose of conservation* isn't old. It's so new that after 10 years of searching I have yet to find more than a few examples of it. I don't mean by this that a lot of underground buildings aren't being built. We hear about them all the time. Look at the Strategic Air Command and the Los Angeles parking structure. A sad commentary on our times is the fact that until just recently most underground buildings were built for the purposes of war, or for additional parking space. Sometimes they underpin a trim little park, but you can imagine how much good that does. Never do we see roofs full of tangled, wild landscapes, waist-deep in wild flowers on rain-saving mulch.

In Philadelphia the rainfall amounts to over 1 million gallons per acre each year. Obviously then, for each acre made impervious by conventional construction, a million gallons of this precious gift are squandered, just as they are at the new shopping center. A million gallons an acre are turned into destroyers of plants and of animal habitats; a million gallons an acre carry to the ocean topsoils, nutrients, and bacteria that enriched the land since long before we learned to pave. Underground architecture can prevent such damage by keeping its paved surfaces hidden from the rain. With a young forest to catch it, some of the rainfall can be held by the rooftop foliage and the deep humus layers, some used by plants and animals on the site, and the rest drained directly to the underground reservoirs now being robbed by conventional construction.

But not all underground structures need have forests above them. In the West, where relatively dry conditions prevail, hardy natural grasses and wild flowers can adorn buildings just as they once adorned the prairies themselves. Parks, farms, meadows—even recreational areas—can thrive on rooftops.

Underground architecture offers us immediate, practical advantages. Because of the earth's rather constant underground temperature (approximating the average *air* temperature at a given location), much less heating and air conditioning is required for earth-covered buildings. Coupled with these savings, the need for almost no outside maintenance, no snow removal, and no lawn sprinkling can further reduce operating budgets. In addition, such intangibles as isolation from both outside noises and atmospheric radioactivity are further incentives to build this way. And the prospect that we may once more find the great, green out-of-doors at every doorstep makes the hoped-for increases in leisure time seem even more appealing.

The only problem is that underground buildings cost as much as, or more than, above-ground buildings. Supporting three or more feet of earth requires quite a structure, and heavy construction is not cheap, at least not initially. It takes energy and environmental crises to show us that dollar costs and true costs are not the same, and that to build the cheap way can be the most expensive.

Even so, the phrase "underground architecture" often tends to repel people. Having been exposed to the depressing look of our subways and tunnels, or to leaky basements and cold, damp caves, they tend to view the real advantages of this new architecture with great skepticism. Most will agree that such land wasters as parking lots and shopping centers should go below ground. And many will even concede that some of our freeways and warehouses and factories belong there, too (in addition to railroads yards, refineries, and museums). But the thought of *living* underground in a windowless, artificial environment is, to them, the ultimate perversion of man's role on earth. Fortunately, most advocates of this new architecture heartily agree.

We were meant to live in the sun and air, to be involved in the seasons, to know night and day. When architects propose windowless, wholly underground buildings they do not include housing. Hundreds of underground houses have been designed, but they always open onto sunny, sunken courtyards or project from the sides of hills so that their rooms can be adequately daylighted. Such underground buildings are perfectly dry and are as sunny as conventional ones.

Man's almost forgotten tradition of earth architecture may now be on the verge of reevaluation.
WILLIAM MORGAN

Energy design has been used as the rationale for esthetic gymnastics like putting buildings up in the air or under the ground.
DONALD WATSON

FIG. 5.1 *The first design for my underground office, Cherry Hill, 1965. The original 1955 office is at left. Fortunately, this one never got built; it would have been a physical and thermal disaster.*

ENTRANCE TO AN UNDERGROUND AUDITORIUM
WATCHUNG RESERVATION - UNION COUNTY PARK SYSTEM
MALCOLM B. WELLS, ARCHITECT/CONSERVATIONIST
AUGUST 1965

SUGGESTED INTERIOR TREATMENT FOR AN
UNDERGROUND AUDITORIUM

UNION COUNTY PARK SYSTEM
MALCOLM B. WELLS, ARCHITECT/CONSERVATIONIST
AUGUST 1965

FIG. 5.2 (above) *Another project that was kind enough to evaporate: a park headquarters building near Elizabeth, N.J., 1965. I knew so little about earth architecture in those days this, too, would have been calamitous.*

FIG. 5.3 (left) *Interior of the park headquarters building. Notice the uninsulated, unwaterproofed exposed rock walls —an invitation to trouble.*

FIG. 5.4 (below) *Reverence for life: a proposal for an earth-covered church, 1964.*

REVERENCE FOR LIFE.....   A SKYLIT UNDERGROUND CHURCH, AT PEACE WITH ALL OF NATURE

AN UNDERGROUND HIGHWAY FOR PASSENGER VEHICLES

FIGS. 5.5, 5.6, 5.7
*Underground highway
proposals, first published by
Progressive Architecture in
1965 and used by permission.*

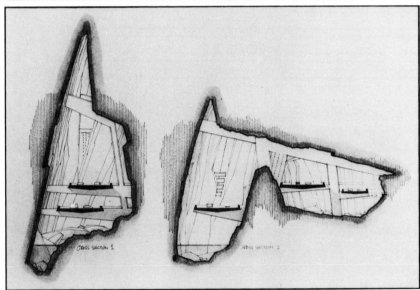

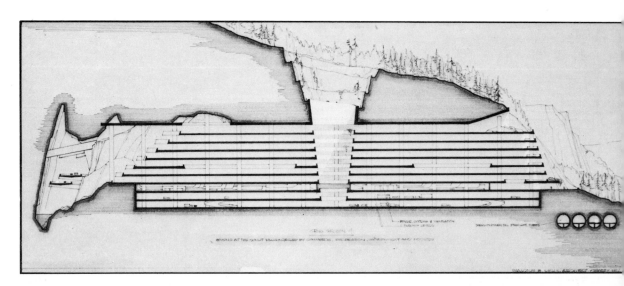

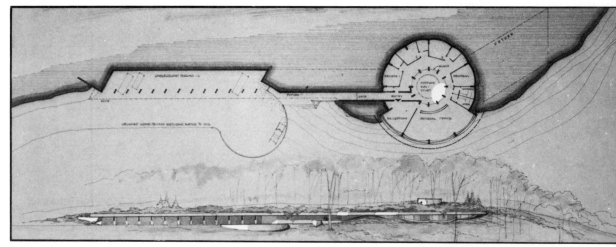

FIG. 5.8 (upper) *Housing, offices, warehouses, factories, highways. A proposal for an underground development, first published by* Progressive Architecture *in 1965 and used by permission. I didn't know about solar heating in those days.*

FIG. 5.9 (lower) *Proposed professional offices at Cherry Hill, N.J., 1974. Never built.*

FIG. 5.10 (upper) *Proposed
underground house at Cherry
Hill, 1964. Never built, it
remains one of the most
popular of my designs. If I were
to build it today I would have
much more south-facing glass,
and would make as many outer
surfaces as possible flat, for
easy application of rigid
insulation boards.*

FIG. 5.11 (lower) *Plan of
underground house at Cherry
Hill, 1964.*

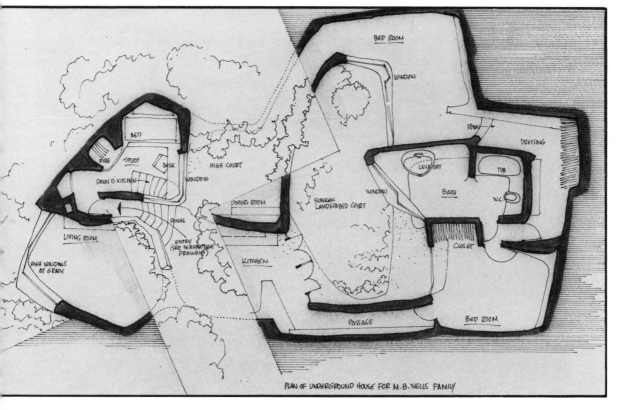

PLAN OF UNDERGROUND HOUSE FOR M.B. WELLS FAMILY

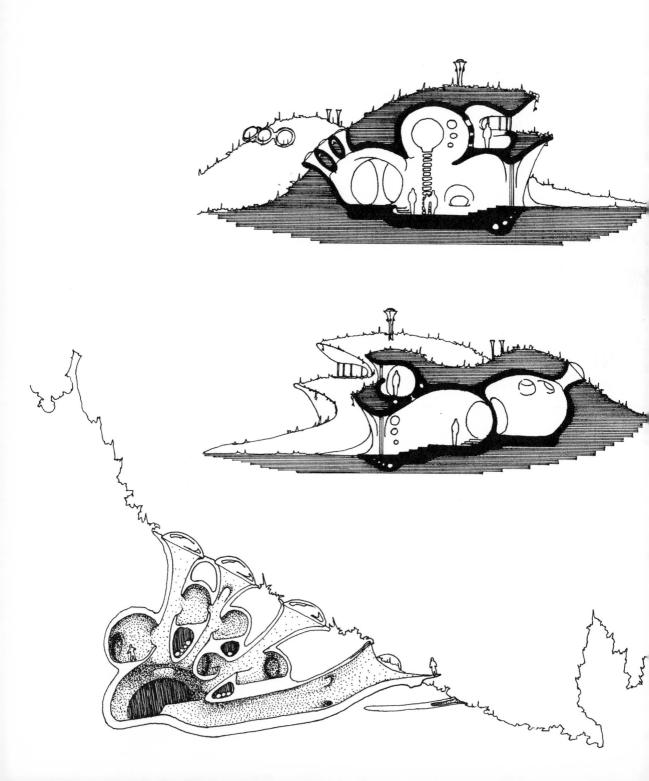

FIGS. 5.12, 5.13, 5.14 *An underground building design by Thomas Sullivan of Missouri, used here with his permission.*

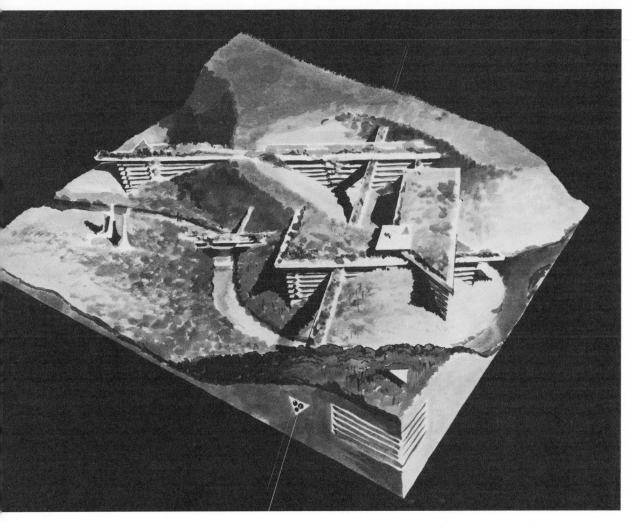

FIG. 5.15 *Proposal for an underground town, 1965.*

FIG. 5.16 *Proposal for an underground suburb, 1965.*

FIG. 5.17 *Cross section through proposed underground suburb, 1965.*

BUILDING THE TRUCK ROUTES AND RAILROADS OF TOMORROW

FIG. 5.18

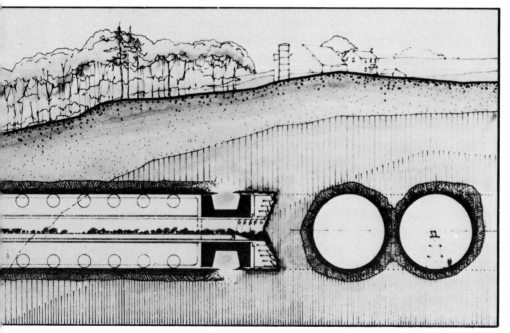

FIG. 5.19 *Before I knew about the horrors of nuclear power I thought that tunnelers with extremely hot collars could fuse structural tubes made of earth, like the stony tubes Darwin discovered which had been made by lightning striking sand. Proposal, 1965.*

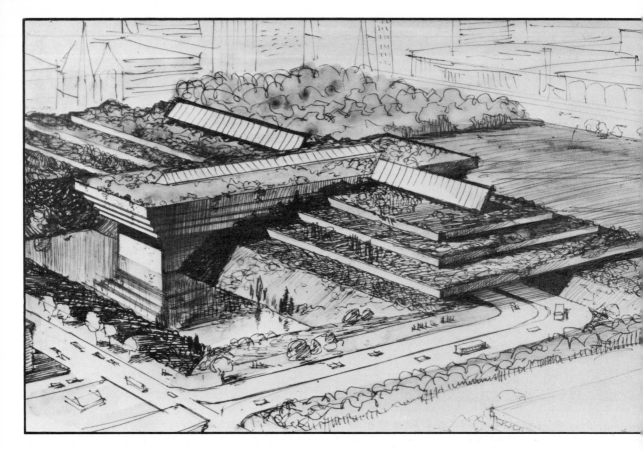

FIG. 5.20 *"The Museum of The Future": Solar heated and earth covered, with percolation beds, underground parking, a wood lot, and on-site waste composting. Done for the American Association of Museums, 1969.*

Whether or not underground architecture will have wide application in the downtown areas of large cities, the fact remains that it has definite applications everywhere else. It offers hope that the great blighted areas around the city centers and along the highways can someday become green and beautiful again. Underground architecture is not a cure-all. It is only one way—one legitimate way—of adapting ourselves to the great life cycle we're now so quickly destroying. Though endorsed by most ecologists and landscapers, the idea has drawn fire from some architects who, misunderstanding it, fear it will create a kind of nonarchitecture. But the idea is gaining popularity each day as people react to the blight all around them.

Some who have built underground have done so for selfish reasons such as security, bombproofing, or the novelty of dialing their own lighting and "weather" effects. If we build for such reasons we're certain to create underground structures as ugly and as destructive as those above ground, but if we do develop a new respect for life—for all the myriad life forms to which we are related—we may just possibly produce an architecture our descendants will treasure.

FIG. 5.21 (upper) *Project for a farm residence by Ray D. Crites, FAIA, of Ames Design Collaborative. 1976.*

FIG. 5.22 (lower) *Environmental Protection Model Settlement 1976. Iowa State University: Ray Greco, Ray D. Crites, K. Kocimsky.*

FIG. 5.23 *The Wildwood School, Aspen, Colorado, 1973. Pielstick, Gibson & Associates, Architects.* (Dave Marlow)

FIGS. 5.24, 5.25 *"The Hobbit House", Alberta, Canada, 1971.* (Jack Bryan, Western Living Magazine)

FIG. 5.26   *Detail, rooftop*
plantings, Moorestown (N.J.)
Municipal Complex, 1976.
Butyl rubber on concrete slab,
earth and deep mulch above.
(Artog)

Cities

Even though I was born in a city (the dingy little industrial town of Camden, New Jersey, just across the Delaware River from Philadelphia), I was raised in the suburbs. I became a suburban architect, married a suburban woman, and raised suburban children. Over the years I did produce some urban froth like a World's Fair pavilion and some retail showrooms, and I designed a law school building for the city of my birth, but my authentic experiences in city architecture have been limited to a few designs for housing, for day-care centers, and for playgrounds in the slums.

FIG. 5.27 *School of Law at Camden, Rutgers University (left), 1972.* (Artog)

The solutions to city problems aren't likely to come from outside med-dlers, and they won't come from the dressing up or beautifying of the mess we've made there. Many of the poor blacks, American Indians, Puerto Ricans, and Mexican-Americans caught inside our cities were born, and in some cases even raised, on farms, far from the asphalt. Many of the unemployed we see lounging on street corners aren't as far from the world of growing plants as we sometimes tell ourselves they are. They probably know more about environmental matters than we design experts do. They have to: they've been forced to live in the worst envi-ronment of all. When city people are given more complete control over their own neighborhoods, I think they're going to show us a thing or two about ecology and about solving environmental problems. After all, the story of life is one of animals depending on green plants, of recycling, of diversity, and of improvisation. The urban poor came from that back-ground. It's the story of subsistence farming as well. There's no hope of a way to feed and clothe and heat great concentrations of city people without reaching far outside their area for the resources involved. But a lot can still be done within that area. Resourcefulness, a subsistence-level background, fuel shortages, vacant land, free sunlight, high food prices, housing shortages—a grinding combination like that might soon gener-ate heartening surprises. Look at the do-it-yourself, low-cost greenhouses Bill Yanda has introduced in the Southwest. They're just a taste of what we're about to see. But what about gentle architecture, underground architecture? Does it have any real application to cities? Isn't it strictly a horizontal, wide-spreading thing, good only for suburban or rural sites? Could whole cities be built underground?

The laws of nature apply with equal force all over the earth. Principles that work in the suburbs can be applied on 177th Street as well as on Winding Lane. But the decisions have not always been left up to archi-tects. Developers and interest rates and building restructions, rather than architects, have established the design directions of these past 10 or 20 years. But look how quickly change is brought about when an oil short-age, a savage winter, or some other crisis appears. The winters of 1977 and 1978 turned millions of people around with respect to solar heating. Ten of thousands have taken a more serious look at earth buildings. As soon as the real pinch begins to pinch, all the old ways go out the win-dow.

We worry about all the barriers to doing things the right way when eventually the right way will not be denied. If we look beyond tomorrow to the day after tomorrow and ask what it's going to be like on that still unspoiled morning, we know it's got to be like this: pro-life, solar, modest, beautiful, waste-free, and simple. The glass towers that make downtown Dayton look so much like downtown Denver and Nashville are bound

A positive, caring alliance between the environmental movement and the civil rights movement is not only possible but necessary. . . . Some people have been too cavalier in proposing policies to preserve the physical environment for themselves while other, poorer people pay the cost.

Advocates of solar and other renewable energy resources have spelled out in policy statements and in actual pilot programs how development of those energy sources would create jobs for unemployed, less-skilled workers.

We need more of that kind of approach.

VERNON E. JORDAN, JR.

to give way to form more expressive of such local phenomena as climate, materials, and tradition.

But the downtown office tower itself will probably be around for a long time. The thing to remember about those prize-winning but interchangeable urban designs is that they're never completely seen. Every tower has tied to it somewhere a parking lot, a power plant, several farms, a chemical factory, dozens of trucks, hundreds of cars, a sewage-disposal plant, some oil wells, and several paper mills. Every New York has its ring of Newarks and Bayonnes. We look with admiration at the soaring glass walls and never smell all the sewage, never feel all the heat losses, never see all the paper being consumed behind those sheer facades. Our capacity for self-delusion seems unbounded, and the crises always catch us unawares.

Gentle architecture may very well never get as far as the corner of Broad and Main, but its influence will. If we manage to survive the nuclear age, the cities of the future are bound to be alive and green instead of dead and gray. We know too much about life priorities now to let the asphalt win. Urban gentle architecture, with heavy emphasis on the use of solar greenhouses, is ideal for the miles of tightly spaced, low-rise housing that ring each central business district. Private, silent, efficient, and secure, as well as hearteningly alive, gentle architecture can not only house high-density populations but provide a good proportion of their food production and waste recycling as well. Our dependence on all the chains of supply and removal now needed to sustain a human settlement is terrifying: one broken link can bring disaster.

Food growing organically on the rooftops and in the greenhouses of the city will reduce that dependence, with an impact felt far beyond the supermarket. From agribusiness and the huge chemical corporations on which it depends, to motor transport and food processing, from sewage plants to investment banks, the consequences are going to be profound, tending to put a more stable base under the precariously unstable thousand-mile food chains on which today's city people must rely and forcing the multinationals to shift their emphasis to more life-oriented occupations.

Urban Mining

Many of the precious resources we took from the surrounding countryside and carried to the city at such great cost still lie there, in and under buildings and in the giant dumps that ring it. Someday, when the more convenient sources of those materials have run out, we'll have to turn to the cities in order to supply ourselves. Already, there are plans to drill for methane in the Jersey meadows (vast dumping grounds outside New York City).

When urban mining begins in earnest we may be forced to build replacement cities, and maybe then we'll try to do everything the right way for a change, starting with transportation and roads.

Cars

There are two things I don't understand about cars. One is how they can smell so good inside and so bad outside. If you're not a walker, a jogger, a runner, or a bicyclist, you may not know exactly what I'm talking about, but all you need do to find out is step outdoors and spend five minutes at any busy roadside. Hikers and cyclists very quickly discover that when they're in traffic, even in light traffic, the smoke from passing vehicles can be almost nauseating. They learn to hold their breath after each car passes until the *second* wave of its double wake has moved past. That long pause in breathing substantially reduces the amount of poison they must inhale.

A few years ago, when I took up bicycling again, I had to learn for myself about the two exhaust waves that followed each passing car. I learned that a lungful of exhaust is the penalty for starting to breathe again before both waves have been felt. This is a precaution that's easy to take in light traffic; the breath pause quickly becomes habitual—automatic. But when traffic is heavy and the double wake of one car is overlapped by that of the next, deep breaths of heavily concentrated exhaust fumes have to be taken. That's when all feelings about the world's number one polluter change from theoretical to gut.

A half-hour's exposure to such traffic will make an environmentalist of anyone. An hour's bike ride starts me on a day of throat clearing and bitter swallowings. Exhaust is vile stuff.

I have spent thousands of hours behind the wheels of cars. I've driven convertibles and sedans, with windows open and windows closed, in light traffic and in heavy, but, aside from the choking fumes I've breathed while driving through tunnels or the clouds of smoke that billow from a few old cars, I can't remember ever having—as a driver—smelled the smells that so infuriate the cyclist. That's what I don't understand: the difference between the inside and the outside car smells. I suppose the fresher-seeming air inside a car is the result of dilution, of a mixing of relatively clean air with the fumes, the mixing action set up as the car moves through the gaseous medium. But that answer doesn't satisfy me. Different cars admit ventilating air at different heights above the road, heights that range from near street level to the tops of windows, and at none of those positions is the vile gas so familiar to the bicyclist ever noticeable while driving. Maybe the difference lies in the depth of breathing required of the foot-powered traveler, in the extra large quantities of poison taken in along with the oxygen. All I know is that the final argument on the subject of the internal-combustion engine lies in the respiratory system of everyone who breathes near a running motor.

The other thing I can't understand about cars is the way the world's largest industry has managed so successfully to keep the tire-noise scandal out of the news. Modern tires are certainly safer than those we had even a few years ago, thanks to steel, glass, and plastic reinforcement, or to tread design, or both. I suspect, however, that all credit for this din we're subjected to must go to the configuration of the tread. As I write these words I can hear the late-night traffic on three different highways, each more than a quarter mile from here. One of them is two miles away. What I hear is not engine noise or transmission noise: it is tire noise, tractive power expressed as sound. Tires leave a permanent nervousness, like an invitation to high blood pressure, hanging in the air. I can hear the energy crisis all night long. I hate to think what it must be like to live on busier streets than mine.

There's a lot of talk about jet noise, and we have laws that require mufflers on engines, but no one seems to talk about muting those other trumpeters, our tires. Can't you imagine the reaction of the rubber makers if a congressional committee began to look into this subject?

"Tread noise? What tread noise?" the tire folks would be certain to say. "We never thought of it as an annoying sound."

Meanwhile, back in Akron, a lot of other rubber people would be racing through their noise research files, checking to see if any damaging medical testimony lay buried there, ready to explode across the nation's headlines, for you can be sure that the members of the tire fraternity are fully aware of the problem.

Paving

Tires come in two parts, of course, a circular rubber part which fits around each wheel of the car, and a hard, flat part attached to the earth. Without the latter, that big rubber doughnut would be useless. I guess I'm more disturbed by the paving than by the tire. The damage done by all our roads and parking lots is incalculable. In fact, as carefully as I've searched I've never been able to find a reliable figure on the ratio of paved area to vehicles in America. When I drive in rural Kansas it's easy to see that the road surfaces must exceed in area, by hundreds to one, the area covered by the cars that use them. But what about New York

In the absence of municipal collection and disposal systems, garbage and trash accumulated in street, alleys, and yards. Horses added their feces to that of the scavenging livestock. Even where street sweepers were available, they would often be powerless in the face of streets that were alternately deep dust, deep mud, or deep snow. The obvious solution to this dilemma was a continuous pavement—hard, smooth, and permanent.

JAMES MARSTON FITCH

City? How much more paving is there in Manhattan than that taken up by all the motor vehicles in the city? Ten times more? If all those legions of taxis, cars, buses, and trucks were carefully parked, bumper to bumper, and side touching side, would they fill only a little corner of the city's asphalt? I suspect they would. I'm just about convinced that no one has any idea how much paving there really is in this country. It's a conviction about which, of course, I would be delighted to find myself proved wrong, but in any case, the area must be enormous. We'd all be a bit more troubled by its enormity if each vehicle had to drag its share of the nation's paving along with it, or even if someone came up with a figure we could use on bumper stickers to show the area of paving tied to each car—something like "This vehicle alone requires 2.6 acres of paving."

We know how to take some of the curse off of paving: by using porous paving blocks; by draining paved areas into retention basins, sunken gardens, and percolation beds, rather than directly into storm sewers; and, best of all, by putting our highways and our parking lots underground. But, all such remedies are ineffective unless they're done at almost a national-mobilization-sized scale, something that land conservation must wait in line many years to see, for a lot of other crises are already lined up behind the big one, the nuclear threat, for national attention. The very best we can look for with respect to the asphalt curse is a paving moratorium. It would at least give us time to repair some of our paving-related environmental damage instead of letting us fall further and further behind as we are doing now.

The great highway-construction lobbies would be up in arms over any cutback in paving work, of course, unless it were done in such a way that no profits or jobs were lost, and there is such a way. It's called super-maintenance. If the skills of the national highway building industry were focused forevermore on nothing but improvements to existing roads, we'd soon have the safest, most functional, and most beautiful highways on earth, and they'd just keep getting better. Under such a program, a gradual move toward environmentally less harmful paving could be accomplished as well, without any additional outlays. Soon we'd have almost no disastrous runoff, no erosion, and, in August, no searing hot parking lots. Better results without the loss of jobs, that's the combination.

This book is about living room—about some of the ways by which we can hope to live together in the future without such great cost to all the creatures, the plants and animals and people, that are vital to our survival and happiness. That's peaceful coexistence in its highest form. It's easy to see that when outdoor space—living room—is considered, the car, the truck, the bus, the driveway, the road, the parking lot, the bridge, and the 50 million *vehicle-related* mines, mills, factories, warehouses, retail outlets, offices, and garages in the United States have an enormous impact. A state-sized slab of asphalt is growing on America. We have 50,000 traffic deaths a year, all-night noise, and a nation going up in smoke.

The car is here to stay, but so, I hope, are we. The problem is not so much to find alternatives to the the private automobile, as it is to extract the venom from it:

Pavement

Accidents

Wasted resources

Dollars going overseas

Smoke and fumes

Noise

Alienation from each other and from the land

Someday, we've got to stop playing with halfway measures and put the car underground. As soon as you consider such a thing, you shift gears mentally. You can't simply bury Detroit's great gift to the world as is. You can't simply build roads that look like the roofed-over nightmare that runs under the United Nations building along New York's East River. This is a roaring slot of blackened concrete, swerving taxicabs and exhaust fumes, far from any resemblance to the covered boulevard its designers must have envisioned. Only on rare occasions, when the traffic is light and you can drive in peace, does the water-level panorama along the East River approach the glory of what FDR Drive might have been. It's in no way a place for the gasoline-powered, noisy-treaded, aggressor-controlled vehicles we have today.

You have to imagine, instead, lightweight electrically powered cars that emit no fumes at all, rolling on smooth, silent treads, cars controlled by a really fail-safe automatic control system. Imagine driving somewhere in such a car, perhaps sleeping part of the way, or enjoying the open panorama beyond the great earthen roof. Imagine nosing your sleek, glassy vehicle into a solar electric socket when you reach your destination, letting the sun recharge the batteries all day, and then rolling silently home again in utter safety. This can really happen if we want it to. The underground highway and the safe, nonpolluting car go hand in hand. But underground highways are as expensive as hell, perhaps five to seven times the cost of conventional ones. Supporting the weight of living land is no simple matter. Megatons are involved. The only way to justify the cost is to have five to seven times as much traffic on a given stretch of road, and that's possible—or will be possible—when automation controls the auto.

Underground highways not only escape the ravages of weather, they release huge chunks of surface land for higher, and presumably more enlightened, use. The very act of going underground forces total redesign of the private automobile, wiping out all its defects but one, the lack of exercise it offers us. And in that regard, I suspect that if we somehow created a more healthful world for ourselves, we would respond to it by getting more exercise, by taking better care of our interior environments.

If we wait for the environmental protection people to save us, however, we'll have to wait a long, long time.

Environmental Protection

The glue of environmental protection has oozed out of Washington, congealed on state capitols, stuck to county offices, and has even begun to give hometown a pasting. Maybe building permits *were* a little too easy to get, back in the sixties, but is this the answer? Pompous little bureaucrats who wouldn't know an acorn from an olive? Review board after review board, staffed with self-righteous do-gooders, all playing the paper game as they work out their frustrations on the natural world? From year to year, from one department to another, even from one board's regular meeting to the next, the rules grow more capricious and more contradictory. They drive the last vestiges of good intention from the participants in the land-use process, turning environmental approval into a legalistic duel in which only the oiliest of the applicants can successfully slip through the cracks. Oh, Earth Day, what hast thou wrought?

This is environmental protection, the paper pusher's paradise. It's all for the good of the environment. It's also pretty good for the people who sell copy machines and blood pressure pills. Meanwhile, your average local field or stream, your friendly neighborhood cornfield, park, beach, or sky, continues to take it on the chin the same as ever. Anyone who knows his way around city hall can get the necessary approvals.

In hundreds of government offices all over America people are doing everything humanly possible to find out not *how few* but *how many* chemicals can be added to the food supply without killing an unacceptable number of us. Legions of pollution-control specialists spend their time monitoring and analyzing our skies and waters, not to see how little smoke and how few chemicals can possibly be dumped there, but rather how much we who breathe and drink can possibly be made to tolerate.

What this all means in terms of animal torture in the environmental protection laboratories will never be known.

The managers of all the nuclear power plants solemnly promise to tell the Nuclear Regulatory Commission about it the minute any deadly (and, of course, invisible) radiation leaks from their buildings, even though the reward for such honesty could be the loss of their jobs. Everyone's looking out for our welfare. We can all sleep in peace.

Viewed from the safety of our homes it all has a kind of ho-hum sound to it. "What's the big deal? They'll find the solutions to all those things. Don't be an alarmist."

But who would have anticipated these massive fish kills along the beaches, or Three Mile Island, or the cancer, years later, that hits asbestos workers, or the mystery diseases that pop up now so unpredictably, or the running out of fuel? At the Philadelphia library, I see that the Encyclopedia of Harmful Substances fills volumes. Over five thousand chemicals are now used in my food, with more being added all the time as manufacturers rush into the highly profitable food-processing industry. Bright new houses blanket a hillside that was an open field the last time we looked.

I don't know what it's like where you live, but many of the streams I've seen in my travels around this country have been straightened to serve as drainage ditches, their banks scarred by erosion, their waters laden with sewage. This is happening in spite of an environmental bureaucracy that's growing as fast as, if not faster than, the other kind of blight. No wonder there's no faith in government, no faith in industry. We're on the cheap-lavish joyride, every new house done in plastic mansion style with walls you can step through, and lucky is the tenant who can find the company that made the gadgets that fail, the plastics that kill, or the windows that leak.

It would be a wise and patient race indeed that could monitor and describe at any moment all the unnatural forces at work upon a given creature. Are these heart-worm pills slowly killing my dog, or is it the heart worms themselves that are slowing him down? I think it's the pills, but I can't be sure. Is this smoky air really hurting my lungs or am I just imagining these chest pains? Does the smoke ever combine with the things they put in my food to form even deadlier combinations? What's that new taste in the drinking water? I suppose I'd be shocked clear out of my skin if I could know the answers to all my environmental speculations, if I could see all of America's environmental mistakes on display. How many chemicals, poisons, rays, and vibrations are at work on me right now? I could study at the finest university and not begin to name them all. Some people say we're better off not knowing; this plays right into the hands of the grand army of the environment, which papers us with trivia while the world dies.

It comes as a surprise to many out-of-state people that New Jersey has a large pine forest across its middle. The Pine Barrens, as that forest is called, are valuable not only for their scenic qualities and wildlife but also as a prime freshwater source. But Philadelphia and Atlantic City are squeezing the Pine Barrens from opposite sides, and the speculators are slicing them up for the kill. Concerned about this threat to the state, New Jersey's Governor Byrne formed an advisory committee to make recommendations for the future of the Pine Barrens and, since no respectable committee of that sort should ever be without at least one gentle architect, I was one of the people he appointed to serve. Naively, I thought we might produce something useful, but after I'd attended a couple of meetings, I could see that we weren't going to make a dent in the problem. The state environmental protection people, well represented on the committee, had their own way of doing things and were unmoved by the anguish of the others. So there we sat, twice a month, meeting to discuss the fate of a tiny oasis in the asphalt desert that already covers much of America's east coast, while each breath we took pushed us that much closer to lung cancer. Talk about black humor—it was like sitting in on the end of the world, being there in such times, for in spite of the governor's admirable intentions with respect to the pinelands, the threat to them was only one facet of an awesome worldwide problem.

When I reviewed the stack of dreary reports sent to me by the Department of Community Affairs before the first meeting, I found agreement on only one thing: the great value of the Pine Barrens. On everything else there was disagreement: over boundaries, state jurisdiction, federal jurisdiction, development rights, zoning, agriculture, housing, industry, recreation. All were up for grabs, and billions of dollars were riding on the outcome. It was the old story of the scalpers versus the preservationists, profits versus land, them or us, and in such struggles the dollar always wins. Vast forces, far beyond those of our little committee, were at work here. Casino gambling, nuclear power, offshore oil, pinelands oil, suburbia. How could we, a group of amateurs—a citizen's advisory committee(!)—hope to stem such a tide? The answer, of course, was that we couldn't; we couldn't begin to.

Nondegradation

The only hope I could see was in the enactment of a single law: "Leave it no worse than you found it." We didn't need a new national park, or a mind-numbing set of environmental standards. All we needed for those

Pine Barrens was just that one line set into law. Then anyone could do what he wanted to do within that limitation. If there were a tough keep-it-no-worse-than-you-found-it law, all destructive housing development would be forbidden, just as would all destructive churches, schools, shopping centers, or refineries.

We have almost within our grasp, today, new ways of using land and natural resources. We're actually on the brink of discovering, or rediscovering, how to develop land without all the negative consequences. Solar heating is an example. Natural—that is, wild—landscapes are another, as are underground architecture, wind power, tidal power, aquaculture, composting, recycling, waterless toilets, and perhaps methane generation. It is conceivable that, as we learn more about these new technologies, thousands of people could move into the pinelands so gently that the great forest would appear to be almost untouched. Remember that another race of people, admittedly in smaller numbers, lived gently in those same Pine Barrens for perhaps ten thousand years. By using what is now called "soft technology," we might create not only buildings but whole villages and towns that would have little adverse impact upon the land. All we need is an incentive, and there, in the pinelands, such an incentive is crying to be born. Keep-it-as-you-find-it legislation would not only protect the pinelands, it would not only retain and expand the tax base, it would not only help to focus national attention on the issue, it would also create huge new labor-intensive industries and new jobs by stimulating the native American genius now so stifled and frustrated by the bureaucratic nonsense through which it must wade in order to invent anything today.

It's hard to imagine a future society that might treat land as shabbily as we treat it. We've got to change in order to survive, not by setting aside areas to be spared from our shortsightedness, but by making *all* land destruction a crime.

I was terribly disturbed by the things proposed at those pinelands meetings: a million dollars for this preserve, 25 million for that. What all the proposed bills and bond issues were, in effect, saying to all New Jersey citizens was, "Go right ahead doing whatever it is you're doing; just don't do it inside these few hundred square miles."

And as for the concept of "nondegradation," it sounded great until I realized that is applied only to certain so-called "critical areas," only to the most remote and unpolluted parts of the Pine Barrens. Was that equal treatment under the law? What about Camden and Newark and Atlantic City? Were they not far more critical areas? What kind of logic is it that justifies dumping the most wastes in the worst places? Why, for instance, were different standards established for different rivers, none of which should have had any wastes dumped into them in the first place?

Nondegradation could have been a first step in the process of saving and restoring that ill-used little state, but the nondegradation of a fragment of an isolated place like the Pine Barrens was pointless; the eight million residents of New Jersey would be allowed to continue to vandalize the surrounding areas until the Pine Barrens were finally choked to death.

Here are my practical definitions of three more terms in the environmentalists' jargon.

SANITARY LAND FILL: Once-beautiful, living land, often life-giving wetland or marsh, now being poisoned forever, buried under an indiscriminate mixture of irreplaceable resources, all with the official blessing of the state.

WATER QUALITY STANDARDS: Standards of filthiness established by state and federal governments. Water is H_2O; it needs no quality standards. What *is* needed is waste management.

POLLUTION CONTROLS: Government-authorized dumping of privately owned wastes into the public domain, a practice that boggles the mind when viewed from a next-century perspective.

The ring of development spreads outward from every town, destroying precious farmland, forests, rangelands, and wetlands. No kind of architecture is going to stop it. We've got to change our values long before we get to the how-to-do-it part. We still have no real interest in, let alone commitment to, the value of land. We're all so spoiled: we feel we should be congratulated if we grow a few vegetables or save paper bags. When we begin to see farming as one of the highest possible human uses for land, then we won't touch it for any lesser use. We'll draw circles around all the cities and say "stop." This is a political and moral decision, not an architectural one. Once we finally agree to stop the killing, we'll turn inward and start to build things the right way, inside the circles, inside the limits we've drawn. How we'll *express* our biological priorities doesn't really matter, although I tend to see city buildings eventually being replaced by earth-covered structures. Step by step, following the rules, we'll begin to put back what never should have been removed in the first place.

No matter where I go, I see cities spreading, suburbs spreading. And I am dismayed to realize that I myself am still a part of it. To me, the eco-architect, smugly saddened by the sight of all those miles of suburbs each time I jet into another airport, it's all junk down there. Land waste. I imagine what it would be like to wipe it all away in a single swipe, never feeling a twinge of regret as houses, factories, highways, schools, and shopping centers are brushed aside. They have no right to be down there killing my American land. But just let someone threaten to wipe *my* house away, and I'd be on the phone to my lawyer and my Congressman. It's a tough question. We all want it to start with the other guy.

Farmland

The more I look into natural systems, the more complex and untouchable I find them to be. Farmland, for instance, isn't just a mass of dark-colored dirt. It's a whole community of soils full of living organisms, nutrients, air, and water, You can't just scrape it aside, build something, and then scrape it all back into place again. Not only the soil itself, but its plant and animal inhabitants, and its drainage, both on the surface and underground, will have been changed, and probably not for the better. If the choice is between building as we build today and building *under* the farm, there is no question about which way to go; almost *any* land-saving option would be better than what we're doing. But if we must build there, then we should build with farming and not architecture, as the priority, perhaps by building linear structures between the rows, spaced to accommodate the largest kinds of farm implements. Maybe the earth-covered ranks of buildings could serve as windbreaks, as shelter belts for the cropland, but the *farmers* would have to make such decisions, primarily on the basis of good farming practices. Then we could begin to think about development profits, and I suppose they'd be quite high, with the prospect of houses, or whole communities, having protected, open farmland at their doorsteps. We've got to start listening to the people who know; not only to the farmer and the biologist but to the many ordinary people whose fund of common sense is so often ignored.

Common Sense

There seems to be a lesson for architects in the reactions of the average citizen to the events around him each day. There's a reservoir of good ideas there that we continue to overlook, much to our sorrow. One of Boston's radio news stations carried the following stories during the course of a single day, back in 1978:

> A massive air and ground search of the Canadian wilderness following yesterday's explosion of a Soviet nuclear-powered satellite has revealed radiation levels high enough to be hazardous to human health.
>
> The U.S. Environmental Protection Administration today launched a long-range program aimed at removing the cancer-causing agents from the drinking water in 35 major cities. The EPA spokesman said he thought this was a major step in the protection of human health.

In the Massachusetts State Legislature, a bottle bill aimed at ending the use of one-way bottles here was stalled by representatives who said 2000 jobs could be threatened by the passage of the bill.

Boston Harbor, which is dangerous to humans and has a deep muck layer of human wastes on its bottom, is again under study. The construction of a new sewage treatment facility has been stalled for years by the Environmental Protection Administration.

Aggravated by today's rains, roofs continued to collapse all across New England under their record loads of snow.

It was quite obvious from the slant of the radio reports that these stories had considerable titillation value, but beyond that they were thought to offer no special commentary on the late-century condition of life here in the United States. Things were different down at the luncheonette, however, and at the post office and in the general store, the average person's judgment having been, if anything, sharpened and not dulled by the day's barrage of ills. The prevailing view on the nuclear accident: "They'd never tell us even if that radiation were spreading all over the country. As long as it's a *Canadian* wilderness they think they can afford a little candor. Those experts think they know more about everything than we do. Can you imagine what this is doing to all the wildlife up there?"

On the subject of carcinogens in drinking water: "Why don't they just pass a law against dumping that stuff into the water instead of taking ten years to build giant treatment plants to take it out?"

On one-way bottles: "There'd be 2000 *new* jobs instead of 2000 threatened ones if the cities weren't choking in our trash. There's broken glass everywhere."

On sewage in the harbor: "Stop pouring sewage into the river; that would solve it. But no, we've got to pay for cleaning up their mistakes after it's too late. It's criminal; the fish don't have a chance."

One collapsing roofs: "It's not the snow's fault. If we didn't build such junk, you could be safe in any building."

In my view, those public responses were right on target. Why is it the average woman or man can see so clearly what is really happening and, more important, why is it that he or she then accepts it with a shrug? Why are our representatives such hacks? Our leaders so spineless? Do politics destroy their judgment? Don't they have to eat and drink and breathe the same things we do?

There is in this a parallel to architecture, and to architects. Now that a lot of people have heard about the alternatives to human wastefulness, they're beginning to insist that we architects provide them. But we are being dragged into righteousness against our will, kicking and screaming, sounding just the way government officials sound when we ask them to do the jobs they were elected to do.

Landscape Architecture

Why does government taint whatever it touches? Here's what I mean:

Having been an architect for so long, I know very well what it is that architects do. But it wasn't until I was exposed to them for a day or more that I discovered where the hearts of *landscape* architects are. Until I found out otherwise, I had thought landscape architecture consisted of finding natural solutions to land-form problems, of bringing a plastic nation back to its senses, and of correcting the mistakes of architects. But you should see what I found when I arrived for a speaking date at a recent convention of landscape architects in the western part of the country.

Two hotel rooms had been reserved for the affair; one, a room little larger than a living room, had been set aside for the meetings; the other, a vast suite, was in the hands of the manufacturers' reps, there to bend the minds of the conferees. Well, so what? I thought; it's all for a good cause. Landscape work needs all the help it can get. I'd expected to see plants, garden tools, and surveying equipment on display. What I actually saw was booth after booth featuring products that were anything but life-oriented. America's petrochemical industry was there in full force, selling everything from fertilizers to pesticides. Pavers, pumps, pipes, and plastics were everywhere. High energy was the theme. Land was the victim.

I was the token environmentalist. Other speakers told of the wonders of improved strip mining, of the problems involved in blasting the newest interstate highway through the mountains, and of the camouflaging of clear-cut timberlands. Dozens of professional landscape architects, most of them now working for the government or for huge companies, were selling their company lines to each other, but not quite looking each other in the eye, either. They were as bad as we are. Pay us enough and we'll do anything.

Here they were, these western landscape architects, the sons and daughters of America's pioneers, now captives of the Forest Service or of the timber, petrochemical, and strip mine companies! Surely, when those landscape architects first went off to college, they'd had nobler goals. Imagine: to landscape the earth! What a high dream to come down from! But, as one of the conferees explained to me later, there never seemed to be a choice. Graduates in landscape architecture could either work for the government or work for big industry. There were virtually no jobs available in private practice. Everyone wound up working for Big Brother.

I am powerfully aware of the fact that, wherever I go, the landscapes that appeal to me are not those designed by landscape architects. My favorite landscapes weren't designed by anyone. They're *natural* landscapes. And I've found in my work with underground buildings that the best landscapes have been those which sprang up voluntarily, with little help from me. Such discoveries always make me wonder if there is any need for landscape architects at all. I know there is, but every time I see a natural landscape, and every time I think about what most landscape architects are doing, I am less convinced that there is a need for the profession. The same, of course, can be said of architects, as Bernard Rudofsky's books show so well. There simply isn't any way to improve on what nature does perfectly well by itself.

Trees

New Jersey's oldest tree is thought to be the one that now stands in a special plot behind an industrial plant owned by a huge multinational corporation. The factory's local management has provided picnic tables, barbecue grills, and even extra parking spaces for those who come to see the venerable oak. All kinds of people, from Cub Scouts and garden clubbers to me, make it one of our favorite stops.

The old tree has a powerful presence; its great, yard-thick arms spread more than just leaves over their tiny plot. Stripped of its habitat, identified, described, commemorated, photographed, fenced, grassed, lightning-rodded, floodlighted, guy-wired, and, for all I know, covered by life insurance, that tough old citizen touches us nonetheless. It helps us measure time. Walt Whitman admired it almost a century ago. It was already a respectable tree when the first Europeans arrived centuries earlier. Born in a primeval forest we can barely imagine, in a confederacy of Indian nations, it grew right out of its time into an era of jet noise and acid rain. We know, when we think about it, that any of the hundreds of pebbles scattered round its giant trunk is older by far than the tree itself. But pebbles don't seem to interest us, not there. It is life and not dead stones to which we respond, there beyond the parking lots and the loading docks.

But how long can a 400-year-old oak expect to survive? Another hundred years? Two? Judging by the number of acorns it produced last fall, it shows no sign of age at all, and acorns, of course, aren't all it produces. Each year, it manufactures thousands of solar collectors — *leaves* — having the capacity to store solar energy in the form of sugar, and starch, and cellulose. Each year, the oak grows larger, holding ever-greater numbers of those green collectors up to the light. Its prospects there for a long senescence seem as good as they'd be in a state park. Maybe even better. No eagle will ever see that tree again, but, barring some unlikely accident, it may well outlive the youngest person now on earth, spending all its waning years the ward of a corporation. No, that oak is in no immediate danger. I'm not going to worry about it.

I do worry about New Jersey's *youngest* tree, wherever it is. Obviously, there's not a chance in a million that I've ever seen it, or ever will, or that I'd know it if I did. There's not a chance in a million that the world's greatest detective could find it. Any of a billion annual seedlings is the youngest tree at any given moment. I don't even know in which of New Jersey's twenty-one counties it grows, but I know that the youngest tree exists, right now, and that it, and the next youngest tree, and the next, will continue to appear as long as there's a bit of soil from which they can spring. Just think, every tree you've ever seen was once the youngest tree on earth!

New Jersey, the most crowded, the most cancerous, the most scorned of states, is shown the way to life each spring by the flag-waving enthusiasm of its tiniest trees. Then we turn around and show them the way to premature death. Early demise is not only a human prospect in New Jersey, it's an animal and vegetable one as well. A shortened life span doesn't make headlines in the natural world, of course, but we may be close to exceeding even nature's tolerance in the Garden State. Natural competitors continue to take their toll of natural creatures, then manmade destruction takes over to finish them off. Not a square foot in all of New Jersey is safe from us; *not one square inch is certain to be left green for even 100 years, let alone for the lifetime of a tree.*

I see New Jersey's youngest tree in every seedling. It seldom occurs to me that this tiny spear here before me could be the *second* youngest of the day, or the 9,643rd. Like other Guinness Book readers, I respond to the superlative.

"Just think" I think, "this tiny poplar about to unfold its very first leaf may well be the youngest of all the billions of trees now growing in New Jersey, and I'm the only person in the entire state fortunate enough to see it." At such times I feel as if I hold the fate of all future forests in these hands. Sometimes, of course, if I'm weeding the vegetable garden, the superlatives are forgotten, and the poplar sprout gets plucked with the weeds; but in the woods, when I drop to one knee before a slender shoot, it's a different story. The heartrending greenness of the youngest tree burns deep into my conscience. It makes me wonder how I can bear to be an architect another minute, knowing as I do what it is that architects do to trees. Sometimes, if I see my youngest of all trees growing from a crack in the concrete, I am utterly transported by the wonder of it all, by the tender power at work there. Vulnerability and toughness—it's a moving combination in showgirl and seedling alike.

When you make rock candy, you heat water to make it dissolve more sugar than it ordinarily would. As long as you maintain the right conditions, the hot, supersweet solution is as clear and sugarless-looking as tap water. But introduce a piece of string at the right moment and crystals will begin to form along the cord. Ideas seem to form in the same way. They don't, apparently, coalesce out of thin air. I was surprised, the first time I saw feathery spears of ice forming on the surface of a November puddle, to realize how like emerging thoughts they were. Something we see or hear or feel acts like the string in the sugary water, releasing from solution the crystals that then may grow at great speeds, along surprising paths, and occasionally beyond our expectations. As an architect, I know better than to grope for an idea in a void. Triggering material has got to be there. When the conditions are right, ideas come tumbling out, sometimes in great detail, far better than anything I could have produced by what might be called "hard thinking" alone. I'm grateful that this process exists. Natural forms seem to unlock ideas I never even knew were there in the jumbled closet of my mind. And it is evident from the architecture of Frank Lloyd Wright that he must have been strongly responsive to natural stimuli.

The point of all this, of course, (getting back to our subject), is landscaping. Planting a few trees in front of the local elementary school on Arbor Day won't solve very many problems. An act like that is too contrived, too far from the reality of asphalt and nuclear power, on the one hand, and the living, green world, on the other. Sometimes, in the mind crystals that start to form when I see a tiny seedling, I see a tree-filled world reappear. Hedgerows—wild ones—start to transect all the parking lots, trees arch to form tunnels over city streets, asphalt turns to beautiful porous paving that can breathe and drink, and I hear birds singing in the city. Suddenly my spirits expand, the way they do when a brisk Canadian high arrives, and I sense a bit of the I'd-forgotten-what-life-was-really-like exuberance that is sure to reward each step we take, away from today's New Jersey, to the new New Jersey that is sure to come. In the meantime, all we can do is learn to handle the details, to find the devices and forms and materials that work, and that have no overriding negative consequences.

Percolation Beds

Percolation beds are an example. Perc beds and retention basins are low areas, usually constructed near impervious surfaces which generate fast runoff. The reasons for building such beds are (1) to do away with the need for large storm sewers, (2) to prevent the further destruction of streams by flash flooding, and (3) to replenish underground water supplies through natural percolation or by the use of charging wells.

If the soils underlying a holding basin are porous, it is usually designed to function primarily as a percolation bed, the instant pond formed by the rain tending to disappear into the soil after a day or two. If the subsoils are not porous, then the low area becomes a retention basin and serves a somewhat different purpose: to hold water until it can run off slowly, through a small drain pipe, into the nearest storm sewer. In addition to the primary reasons for having such a basin, there is also the advantage of reduced construction costs; drains for retention basins need no expensive, oversized pipes. One variation on the retention basin, where earth strata far below the basin floor have good percolation, is to use charging wells: to drill shafts through the intervening impervious layers, to fill the shafts with stone, and to let them channel the surface water directly into the deep earth. (The pollution of deep, water-bearing layers is of prime concern in this case, however, for much of the surface runoff from highly populated areas contains materials like dog droppings, cigarette butts, motor oil, and asbestos fibers, all of which could go straight down the shaft

FIG. 5.28 *Construction Fasteners, 1976. Percolation bed twelve years later.* (Artog)

and into the water supply. Obviously, extreme care is needed before one tampers with earth resources in that way, and only already-clean water should be allowed into such wells.)

There's hardly any limit to the forms that retention basins can take, although economics usually dictates that the pits be rectangular, with sloping sides. I've seen retention basins and percolation beds that were circular, irregular, long and narrow, and a lot of other shapes. One was an abandoned quarry. The nicest ones had one thing in common: they were beautifully landscaped.

The best landscapes are the ones that evolved pretty much by themselves. After all, in most places all you have to do is add mulch to earthbanks and let nature do the rest. Local wild flowers stand ever ready to move in and do their spectacular job. In Belgium I saw small valleys filled with poppies and waving grasses. Those wild gardens, which had been designed to take the runoff from expressway interchanges, were so nicely in tune with the surrounding countryside they seemed to have been always a part of it—natural depressions in a rolling land. It was only after I saw a contour map of the highway slopes, and saw the carefully engineered grades, that I knew what had been done.

Percolation beds and retention basins can very quickly fill with water during a heavy rain. Children playing there could drown if the beds were improperly designed. Like all other man-made structures, perc beds or retention basins can be dangerous if proper precautions aren't taken to assure public safety. When the side slopes are gentle the water will rise relatively slowly, and escape is easy. In more crowded areas, where the sides must be steeper, there should either be gently rising escape ramps, or the entire area should be fenced, off limits. Fencing, however, is usually a sign of failure, of poor design; and overfencing can even further dull our fast-disappearing animal alertness. It can lead to the kind of society in which, eventually, everything from the canyons of the West to the curbs of the East is fenced and handrailed into hazard-free dullness. We can't eliminate all the hazards without becoming even more creampuffy a people than we already are.

The size of a percolation bed depends on the size and nature of the watershed upstream or uphill from it, with some extra capacity figured in to accommodate the possible added runoff when some of the still-green areas upstream are paved. The size also depends upon the percolation capacity of the underlying soil, and the amount of rain likely to fall in any given number of hours or days. There are a lot of "what if" considerations as well. What if the porous layer of earth underlying the bed were frozen solid and a violent rainstorm occurred? What if the bed or its drainpipe were choked with snow and ice, or mud, or debris, and a cloudburst decided to happen?

The architectural possibilities of earthscapes are unlimited. Done in the spirit of the site, they can help make an acceptable piece of gentle architecture into an outstanding one, and they make possible a far wider selection of building sites. When people come to me and ask for help in the selection of sites for their new buildings, I usually tell them something like this:

Site Selection

For many years, whenever new clients asked me what to look for in selecting a suitable site for a building, I responded by offering them lists of good or bad points, or by giving them sketches showing various site features. These are typical. Everything said on the sketches is true, but,

FIG. 5.29

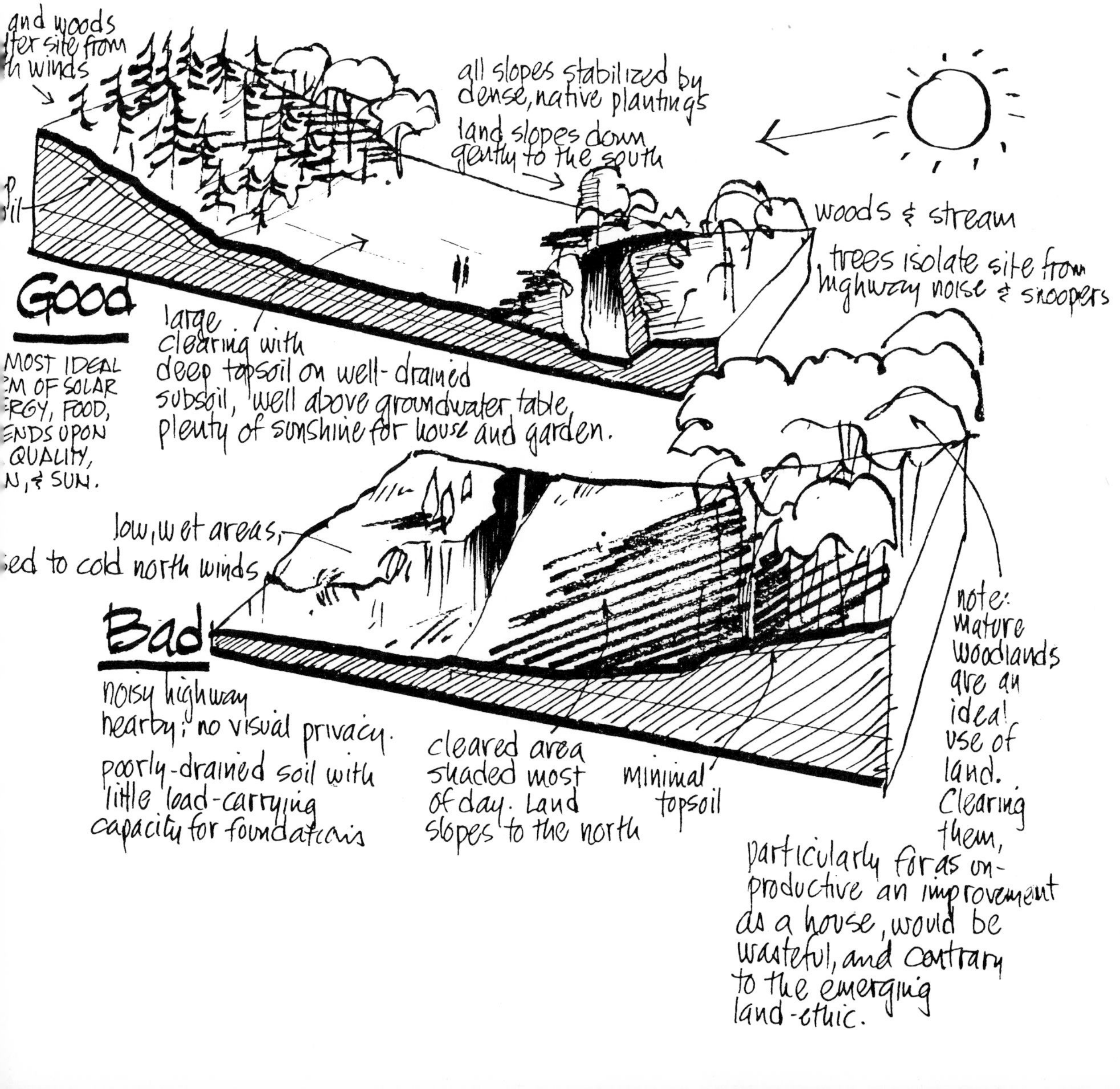

and woods
ter site from
th winds

il

all slopes stabilized by dense, native plantings
land slopes down gently to the south

woods & stream

trees isolate site from highway noise & snoopers

Good

MOST IDEAL
M OF SOLAR
RGY, FOOD,
NDS UPON
QUALITY,
N, & SUN.

large clearing with deep topsoil on well-drained subsoil, well above groundwater table, plenty of sunshine for house and garden.

low, wet areas,
ed to cold north winds

Bad

noisy highway nearby; no visual privacy.
poorly-drained soil with little load-carrying capacity for foundations

cleared area shaded most of day. Land slopes to the north

minimal topsoil

note:
mature woodlands are an ideal use of land. Clearing them, particularly for as un-productive an improvement as a house, would be wasteful, and contrary to the emerging land-ethic.

over the years, I grew less and less willing to see someone buy a valuable site simply for the purpose of having it destroyed by another of my buildings. It took me a long time, but I finally discovered that almost everything I'd ever been taught about site selection was wrong. That's when I began speaking, to anyone who would listen, about building on already-ruined land, on strip-mined areas, on worn-out farmland, or on old parking lots. I soon became so eloquent on the subject that I talked myself into building on such a site. It was a tiny, 5000-square-foot lot: an eroded, partly asphalted patch of land, squeezed between a six-lane highway and a polluted stream. And there, to my relief and delight, I found that the claims I'd been making with regard to the restoration of such sites were, in fact, actually true.

A year after the building was completed and covered with subsoil and mulch, the site had become almost a jungle of wild flowers and wildlife—without the introduction of any topsoil! Even better results would have been gained through the compost-enrichment step recommended by Portland architect David Deppen: "The most rewarding action for a homeowner would be to begin with a worn-out, eroded, treeless site and then nurture it back to health, planting ground covers, windbreaks and native plants, and gradually building up deep soil by composting." I never did any composting, but nature forgave me anyway.

If you want an ideal building site, tell the realtor to show you his worst. What a rich life you'll have, if he gets it for you, undoing that little bit of civilization's damage.

Site Selection Failure

But I had to eat those words after I'd searched for a place on which to build my new house and office on Cape Cod. It was another case in which my theories were at odds with reality. No worn-out land was available. I went to almost every realtor in the area. I toured the countryside. I visited tax offices and got the names of the owners of promising-looking pieces of eroded or otherwise spoiled land, but I was absolutely unable to buy any. First of all, realtors had almost no such properties listed, and the owners I approached were in most cases holding their worn-out parcels for investments, as hedges against an uncertain future. Some admitted that their gravel pits, or their old parking lots, were in the path of a future highway, that they expected to make killings within a few years. They weren't aware of the killings they were already making by leaving their land in such condition. The three worn-out sites actually for sale—a gravel pit, a bankrupt little shopping center, and a farm—were all zoned "commercial," off limits to houses. So Shirley and I had to build in the woods, just like everyone else, hoping that the fast healing of land wounds we've been able to encourage elsewhere in the past will take place there as well.

Gentle architecture is not a description of the way things are, but of the ways things can be. My site-selection problems offer another illustration of the distance we still have to go. The site we bought is beautiful, typical, Cape forestland—mixed pine and oak. Pitch pine and scrub oak. The soil: sand, under a few inches of loam. Surprisingly, in view of the poor nutrient value of the land, there's a lot of wildlife in the area, and we are determined to build in such a way that, within a few years, not only will the forest have been restored but the land and its creatures will have been enriched as well.

Should you bet on that happening? Judging by the record, I wouldn't trust any architect's claim, but my score has been getting better. The health of the last few sites with which I've been involved has now improved beyond all my expectations. I couldn't be given better encouragement.

CHAPTER SIX

Energy and Resources

I don't know what made me think of my journal today. I hadn't thought about it, or even made an entry in it, for months. But when I opened it near the middle and began to read, the great winter of 1976–1977 came rushing back with a vengeance: tankers breaking up in savage storms raging across the North Atlantic, millions out of work as factories shut down, oil barges icebound in the Ohio River, water mains bursting, uncontrollable fires, deaths by freezing, immense fuel consumption, spiraling prices, thousands of cars abandoned, blizzard following blizzard, cities isolated. Reading about it all again touched off a deep shiver in my soul—a death fear, I suppose.

I remember when I made those entries. I sat huddled in the warmest corner of my house, layered in long johns and sweaters, the thermostat set right back to 50°, the oil burner laboring endlessly in spite of it, and I cursing myself for having designed so many stupid buildings over the years, imagining what it must have been like aboard a tanker on such nights, and cursing myself for having helped cause disasters at sea.

I had felt differently in 1962. That was the year *Progressive Architecture* had published that same house, and *House Beautiful* had made a cover story of it. That was the last year of our innocence: Kennedy still alive, Vietnam unknown, moon landings a myth, nuclear power still a vague future threat, and fuel oil galore. What a difference the next 15 years were to make! They forced us all to grow up a bit, and to think about consequences for a change.

But how slowly we react! Turning the construction industry around is like trying to stop one of those supertankers. It takes miles to brake a giant ship once it's under way. Here we are, already designing the buildings of the early eighties, and we still don't have our values in order. Take the chimney and the fireplace, for example.

Chimneys have long been suspected of being energy wasters, but the appeal of a log fire and the industrial symbolism of a smoke-belching factory chimney still blind us to the breadth of the scandal. Enormous amounts of energy get lost up chimneys. Obviously, all the heat and

Around 40% of our national energy consumption is used in the building sector to heat, cool, and illuminate our buildings; to manufacture building products; and to construct buildings.
DONALD WATSON

Most estimates put the amount of energy which is consumed in residential and commercial buildings, for all purposes, at around 33% of total U.S. energy consumption.
PHILIP STEADMAN

Indigenous and vernacular building at its best is a direct expression of adaptation to climate and to the constraints of resources.
DONALD WATSON

waste materials they release are lost to any useful purpose, and even when the boilers and fireplaces are idle, chimneys continue to draw hard-won heat from every room in their vicinity, venting energy to the open sky.

Chimneys and Fireplaces

More efficient chimneys no longer rely on conventional dampers to prevent this loss. They come with tight-fitting top-of-the-flue caps as well. And, because even the metal flashings around chimneys are now known to be heat bleeders, we're learning to insulate those treacherous components, too. Infrared photographs of buildings in wintertime show dramatic telltale glows from the bands of flashing around uninsulated chimney bases, room heat escaping by way of this conductive metal and its air-leaking joints.

Someday, we may learn to capture and use all the products of combustion, not just a fraction of the heat as is the case today. When that happens two great architectural features, the chimney and the open fire, may bite the dust. But that's still a long way off. House design has always centered on the open fire and the great masonry chimney piercing the roof. We won't let them go without a struggle. But the sun must eventually become the central fire in the house. Already, fireplaces are being replaced by the far more efficient, albeit often troublesome, airtight wood stoves. The fireplaces that remain are moving behind glass, their combustion air carried directly to the fire chamber by means of insulated ducts from the out-of-doors. The appealing, walk-in fireplaces we associate with the kitchens of Colonial times are well on their way into the history books. Skies and forests may be rejoicing at all this but living rooms must mourn the chill that's come over them with the lost prospect of roaring fires on cold winter nights. We draw only small comfort from the fact that for woodstoves there are now only one or two logs instead of the former ten or twenty to carry to the hearth each day.

We shudder at the ugliness of many solar and wind-powered devices, failing to realize that if fireplaces and chimneys had never been invented they'd seem just as strange, suddenly appearing on the scene, as the solar devices of today. Obviously, a lot of ugly fireplaces and grotesque chimneys had to be tried and rejected before the generally accepted classics we now love entered the human tradition. Hang on; we'll get there.

The subject is far from resolved. Reactionaries continue to insist on their right to burn wood wastefully. Purists forgo the magic of the flames. Inevitably, someone will come along with a videotape of a crackling fire, and the smell of woodsmoke will be offered in spray-can convenience. But the best bet so far seems to be that of having, on occasion, a modest-sized open fire, having most of its combustion air furnished directly from the out-of-doors, and having the fire in a fireplace so cunningly designed that it will extract most of the chimney heat in the form of warm air or warm water, the energy in either of which can be stored for later use. Good designs are seen now and then, but we are still far away from the efficient and beautiful fires of the future. Meanwhile, we can save a lot of energy by lowering thermostat settings in the wintertime. But let's not kid ourselves. Many of the people who rave about the benefits of living with low wintertime thermostat settings have done so to the annoyance, if not the downright discomfort, of others in their households. We have not yet learned how to create varied yet dependable temperatures within a given space, and the deficiencies of heating systems must be made up for by the addition or removal of clothing.

Unfortunately, however, there are practical limits to that kind of compensation. Many people, and I don't mean just the very old or the disabled, cannot be comfortable under prolonged exposures to 60-, 62-, or even 65-degree room temperatures, regardless of the amount of clothing worn. (There are, of course, those who refuse to dress for the season, but theirs is not an architectural problem, and it cannot be solved here.) It's quite true that considerable amounts of energy are conserved by lowering room temperatures, but it's also true that we seldom hear from those on both sides of the comfort question. As long as environmental considerations are fashionable, the Spartans will continue to have our ears. But is that what we want? Is an architecture acceptable only to the fitness crowd the only kind to have?

Comfort

Grandmother Voigt is 96 years old. She seems to have grown smaller in the last few years, but in some ways she's as pretty as ever. At times it's hard to tell if she's 96 or 196. Her skin seems almost transparent. She moves with a mixture of deliberation and grace, and she's cold in rooms any cooler than 80 degrees. Can I look her straight in the eye and tell her that an architecture I choose to call gentle requires that she submit not only to 70-degree but to 65-degree temperatures as well? If I can, then we have made a very strange kind of progress.

Properly insulated buildings can be warmed to *any* desired temperature, even when solar energy is the only heat source. We've been misled by all this 65-degree talk. It need apply only to existing structures in which massive energy-saving steps have not been taken. In such buildings, the 5- or 10-degree difference from former temperature settings can mean a lot in dealing with high fuel bills. But a proper architecture, a life-centered, *gentle* architecture, must be based on life needs, and if Grandmother Voigt needs 80 degrees then that is the temperature for which her quarters must be designed. Done properly, they'll require little or no additional fuel.

There's a lot of confusion today in energy-and-architecture circles as to what does and does not constitute high technology. The popular view is that solar heating and wind power are representative of low technology, while SSTs and glassy office towers are high. But I wonder if it really is high technology to burn enormous amounts of fuel in order to fling tourists across oceans, or to heat naked buildings. Like many other modern labels, the high and low of technology seem here to be applied in reverse. It is possible that this was intentional? High certainly sounds better than low, but look at the wild world. Look at your own hand. That it will not only perform incredible feats but also repair itself, and run on little more than bread and water, if necessary, for decades, puts to shame all "high" and "low" technology.

If you think it's hard to get a plumber or a doctor at 2 A.M., think what will happen when the computerized house of the future blows a fuse! We stand squarely between the two technologies, whatever your choose to call them, able to draw the best or the worst from both worlds. Solar heating and sewerless toilets no longer mean wildly unpredictable temperatures and backyard privies. By drawing from the best of both the scientific and the natural worlds, we can have comfortable, dependably stable temperatures and waterless indoor toilets in our homes today.

That, in my opinion, is one of the two big challenges in architecture over the next generation or so: find better ways without sacrificing comfort. The other challenge, of course, is to make the new architecture appealing; to make it beautiful and well proportioned, and appropriate and honest. We haven't even begun to find the limits to architecture.

Insulation

Most of Cape Cod's soil is ordinary sand. Growing in it, over most of the Cape, is a forest of pitch pines, beautiful trees with such perfect carelessness of grace, each one seems almost to have been designed by a great Japanese artist. On the sand, under the pines, there is a thick layer of pine needles, dried to a rich, tobacco brown. To walk on them barefoot, after one's soles have been toughened a bit, is a kind of luxury not yet offered by Bigelow, and to smell them is to smell everything that's still wild and clean about pine forests everywhere. It makes my dog smell almost like a woodland spirit, and I suspect that deer and all the other pineland creatures must smell that way as well.

One night last winter, after several weeks of cold weather, five inches of wet snow fell on the Cape. They fell, plunk, in heavy silence. In the frosty morning sunlight, five inches of gleaming perfection were carried on every part of every pine, leaving a great, brown bed of needles on the ground below. It was so picture-perfect it missed being cheap calendar art only by a hair; each laden branch was done with heart-stopping perfection. Where there were no trees, the ground was evenly covered: five inches of brilliant whiteness were draped over every fold and wrinkle of the frozen land. As the sun rose higher, soft, plopping sounds could be heard, as branch after branch shed its load. The snowless circles of needles beneath the trees, so perfect at dawn, were soon spotted white from the tiny avalanches. It was noon before the snow had completely melted anywhere, and the first areas to be exposed were not patches of earth. They were of pine needles, not the already-exposed areas of needles under the trees, but rather the needles in the snow-covered areas *between* the trees. By the end of the day it was obvious that the snow stayed longest on bare earth, it having long since melted from the needle-covered areas. My first thought, in trying to understand what had happened, was that the early sunlight, in shining down through the translucent snow, had reached the dark brown needles and warmed them enough to do some additional melting from below, but far darker-colored areas of snow-covered *soil* had exhibited no such tendencies.

Insulation must have been the contributing element, insulation working in two ways: first, the needles had held the last of autumn's warmth in the ground, protected from the freezing winds, and were now letting that stored-up warmth help melt the snow from below; and second, the fallen needles had prevented the bottom-chilling of the snow that the exposed and frozen soil had allowed.

It's easy to see, when looking at the roofs of houses after a blizzard, which ones are poorly insulated. Heat loss through unprotected roofs quickly melts the snow away. But the pine-needle phenomenon seemed to fly in the face of such theories. In the woods the insulation helped melt the snow!

The difference, apparently, is in the heat *sources*. The surface of the earth out-of-doors is heated from the outside, heated by the sun and the sun-warmed air. If Cape Cod's soil had been warmed primarily from below, by the internal heat of the earth, for instance, then the first areas of snowmelt would have been those above the areas of exposed earth, and the pine-needle-covered areas would have slowed the escape of interior warmth enough to hold the snow blanket a bit longer.

None of this may have any direct bearing on architectural insulation, but it's a good reminder not to make too many blind assumptions about the flow of energy until all the factors have been considered. And, even when they have been considered, experts often draw different conclusions. On the subject of underground buildings, for instance, there is a minor controversy as to whether the floor should be insulated from the underlying earth. One theory suggests that the earth below the floor slab will act as a very helpful thermal reservoir in storing the heat conducted downward into the soil. Others, including me, feel that the floor of an underground building should be insulated because the earth, never quite attaining the warmth of the room, will act as an immense heat sink, slowly but endlessly drawing warmth from the floor slab, and causing foot chill. I happen to know, from the direct experience of cold feet, that this phenomenon does occur in some underground buildings in which floor slabs have been left uninsulated. Still, it's a lot better to have a reservoir of 65-degree earth, below and outside an underground building, than a reservoir of 55 degrees, so a successful compromise might be to do without the insulation outside the lower half of an underground structure, but to use heavy, insulating area rugs underfoot, particularly at seating areas where the feet are likely to be in contact with the slab for extended periods, and to insulate with wall hangings near such locations. The wall panels will slow body-heat radiation to the cool walls but will allow room-heat absorption by the wall/earth mass. In the summertime, when a radiant cooling effect is desired, the hanging panels can be removed, allowing the body to beam its unwanted warmth into the walls for safe-keeping until cooler weather.

As we become more aware of the thermal phenomena around us we can expect to find insulation doing far more sophisticated jobs. Until then, the best practice is to insulate everything that feels cold in the winter and thus to slow this storm of energy that rises from every human settlement.

The Fairchild F-127 is one of the few, perhaps the only, high-wing aircraft with two-and-two seating now operating commercially in the United States. I love to fly in it. Not only does it offer a view of the ground unobstructed by any wing, and a view of a giant landing gear assembly being retracted and lowered only a few feet away, it also keeps alive that favorite question of mine about the wheels of big airplanes: why in the world doesn't it pay to install a small motor to start them spinning before each landing, rather than let these huge and, I'm sure, terribly expensive tires smash into the ground at speeds of anywhere from 100 to 150 miles per hour? The spin-motor could probably even be wind-powered and help to slow the airplane a bit. It's a question that's puzzled me for so long I almost dread hearing the answer. It's probably so dumb and obvious that it would embarrass me, like, "What if only the left side worked and we hit the runway with one wheel spinning and one not?" Still, *every* objection I can imagine could be overcome, if not with such proven cure-alls as sewerless toilets and solar energy and underground architecture, then with some other item of good old American know-how.

But that's not the subject at hand. Something else I saw from the window of an F-127 in which I was flying recently commanded all my attention. Kept from landing because of other traffic in the area, the pilot announced that we would be in a holding pattern for 5 or 6 minutes, and informed us that those passengers seated on my side of the aircraft would have a good chance to see some tankers for carrying liquefied natural gas being built at a shipyard below.

It was wintertime. The ground was covered with snow from a recent storm. Even then, a week later, most of the ground was still white. So was the shipyard. Only the work areas had been cleared. Then I saw the ships, five of them, each with its huge spherical tanks in different stages of completion, the curved steel plates still in dirty shades of brown and yellow.

We were flying at about 3000 feet, but I could see tiny human figures and the blue-white flames of welders' torches on the frozen ways below. Superficially, it was an interesting, even dramatic, glimpse of a giant industry that few of us ever see, but on a deeper level it was a picture of potential disaster in the form of tanker explosions which, if they are anything like the predictions, will be second only to those of nuclear bombs. There was tragedy, too, in the waste of precious resources implied by those half-finished vessels. America is rushing more and more tankers into service in order to suck the world dry of its natural treasures a little bit faster. Anything, appearently, rather than conservation. I could hear my next lecture taking shape inside my head, and I cursed myself for not having brought along a camera, even though the drama below us would have shown up as little more than a few faraway dots on the screen.

As we continued to circle, my attention drifted from the shipyard to the other areas over which we were circling: a coal-burning power plant, spilling its gray plume of smoke into our sky, the oily waters of the bay, the familiar brown sky of North America, and the depressing-looking houses that stretched away in all directions, dark and dirty-looking in contrast to the snow.

Dark! It hadn't soaked in until then. Every roof was free of snow. Every one. Snow was on the ground, but none was on the roofs. It was proof of more fuel waste than I'd believed possible. I'd seen side-by-side houses on which snow had long since melted from only one, in which case it was obvious that one had simply been underinsulated. But *thousands* of houses? Could they all be underinsulated? Maybe the sun had melted the snow from them before it had cleared the ground. There was no sunshine to give me a north direction, but a check of only a few houses was enough to show me that none of the roof surfaces, not even the sunless slopes, were still covered. Only a few porch tops and garage roofs remained white. My next theory was that the snow had slid from all the roofs. Theory number two was shattered by a view of a local shopping center. Its vast flat-roofed areas were snowless, too.

I just didn't want to face the obvious, the fact that none of those buildings was properly insulated and that all were fuel wasters, so I spent more time than I should have spent in trying to invent other ways to account for the mysterious disappearance of rooftop snow. Sudden rain? There had been none. Violent winds? But there were no drifts in sight. No, there was only one answer, and it led right back to those half-finished tankers. The whole story was there in two nutshells: fuel supply, fuel waste. It was hard to believe that intelligent creatures were actually caught up in anything that expensive, that self-defeating, and that destructive. Because of incompetent builders and architects, those tankers were being built. Because of the tankers, our skies would get smokier, fuels would get scarcer, and horrendous explosions were almost certain to make banner headlines.

If the money being spent on the tankers and the fuel they were to carry were spent on insulating those houses, there'd be far more people employed, there'd be vast and permanent fuel savings, and there'd be a satisfying drop in the outward flow of U.S. dollars. Ah, but if that kind of thing caught on, the United States would soon be using only 90 percent of the fuel it uses today, and how could the energy companies explain that to their stockholders—especially if the trend promised to continue in a downward direction? Gentle architecture could put a serious crimp in the profits of some of our largest companies. And what would happen to our economy then? My prediction: boom. As the dollar strengthened so would everything else.

But how does an unskilled homeowner make an old building energy-efficient? Sure, an architect or a builder with plenty of free time, a lot of money, and a determination to spend weeks renovating the place might be able to do it. But things don't work that way. Am I kidding myself about insulating all those aging buildings? How could it be done?

One building at a time. Why not subsidize energy *conservation* instead of energy production? Every building owner would become a conservationist overnight if paid to be one. Millions of people have already demonstrated that it doesn't take an architect or a builder to insulate a building. With suitable encouragement many others can do it as well.

Rats, Roots, and Termites

Owners might have trouble with rats and roots and termites if they tried to insulate foundation walls without taking the proper precautions. Most buildings perform better, thermally, when their insulation is on the outside, and this practice, when applied to underground, or earth-sheltered structures, may tend to invite trouble. On any such job, sooner or later I'm sure I'll hear about roots that have penetrated the waterproofing materials behind the insulation layers. The root-damage potential, particularly in underground buildings, probably generates more questions than any other.

So far, I can say only two things in response. One is that roots are not supposed to go through waterproofing layers. Horticulturists say roots will normally go only where there is water, and if water does not penetrate the membrane, then the roots will have no motive to penetrate it either. My other comment is that I have so far, in my decade or so of earth-cover experience, never encountered a problem with roots. Not that there won't ever be one. I'm sure that root hairs will grow through the tiny cracks between the insulation boards, seeking that film of water that lies beyond, there between the boards and the waterproofing material on the outer surface of the structure. It's a warm, moist space of the kind that roots, if I understand them at all, would go for. But the problem is not one of root filaments, of tiny root hairs growing behind the insulation panels. The problem is that of the larger roots that would soon develop. Where there were root hairs yesterday, there can be thin roots today and giant roots tomorrow, tending to pry the insulation boards away from the wall, allowing more water to get behind the panels and against the vulnerable building wall, thereby decreasing the effectiveness of the insulation itself.

I'm not sure that the owner of a building would even be able to detect this phenomenon if it were occurring. The building would become somewhat harder to heat, over the years, but that could be blamed on many other factors. We still have quite a bit of research to do. (Research is my cover-up word for trial and error, for mini-disasters and mini-triumphs, and for doing it the right way next time.)

This root business is closely related to the rodent problem, but I'm still not sure how serious a problem it will ever be. So far I have found it to be relatively slight.

My New Jersey office had sheer courtyard walls, seven feet straight down from grade, and they turned out to be a hazard to small animals. Now and then, when I arrived in the morning, I would find dying or dead rabbits, rats, mice, and even turtles in the sunken courtyard. Why they fell, or jumped, I'll never know. Before I saw them, I had always assumed that wild creatures needed no protection from vertical drops, that they were so used to the hazards of the natural world that warnings at the edge of a sunken courtyard would not be necessary. So I learned another lesson, at their expense.

Insulation on the outside surfaces of buildings seems like an invitation to small animals which might consider that soft material an ideal place in which to make warm nests. But, as I said, so far my buildings appear not to have had this problem. One reason for my good luck may be the fact that, on every building of that type, I've covered the exterior insulation with a hard layer of cement plaster on metal lath, and have extended that skirt of protective plaster at least three feet below the finished grade. My theory is that the plaster will discourage, if not prevent, both rodents and roots from getting into the soft insulation behind it. But I'm sure that, as the years go by, I will continue to be surprised and chagrined by new discoveries involving natural forces and natural creatures.

Termites pose another threat. They can easily go through the soft, insulating layers on the outer surface of a buried building, and I suppose that they will do so if there is any reason for them to. If untreated wood is buried within the plane of the insulation it certainly would be vulnerable to them. Careful detailing rather than resorting to poison seems the more responsible course to take. Each feature of a building should be thought of as the target of various pests and environmental forces, and then arranged so as to avoid contact and conflict as much as possible. That is the best way to practice: hours of forethought preventing months of heartburn.

North-Sloping Sites

Solar-heated buildings are said to be most efficient when they face southward. This seems to create a problem for anyone who owns a north-, or east-, or west-facing slope and wants to take advantage of solar heating. But it is a fact that unless your site slopes steeply in the "wrong" direction, you can still create a solar opening facing to the south, regardless of your building's location or its orientation on the site. Many buildings on north-facing slopes, buildings that actually front on streets to the north of them, have solar openings, great sky windows, or solar collectors, facing the other way—toward the south; This arrangement can be just as effective as the reverse—where the whole building faces the other way. As a matter of fact, there may be certain advantages to sites that don't face southward. One is that they can offer a better view in that direction. Also, colors are more intense—more pleasant—because everything is front lighted, not back lighted as is everything you see to the south of you.

Windows on the south side of a building admit a lot of free energy, but they also mean glare, smudges, and squinting, which can be terribly annoying and require a lot of window washing. I suppose the ideal design would be one in which south-facing solar panels or solar windows admitted heat energy to a building, but in which all the view windows—small ones, to be sure—faced north. That would be a winning combination.

The worst drawback of a northward land slope is in its shortening of the outdoor growing season. If a site at, say, St. Louis (39° north latitude) slopes 5° to the north, then the solar exposure of that site is more like that of New Hampshire (44° north). You get less sunlight on the garden, and, unless you employ some countermeasures, the growing season is much shorter as a result. One appropriate countermeasure is the use of windbreaks to slow the chilling winds from the north and northwest sides of the property, and still another is the use of reflectors (white-painted walls, shiny metal, canvas panels) to bounce extra sunlight onto the northern slope.

(If you live south of the Equator, of course, you should exchange north for south in everything I've just said.)

When it comes to views, and to windows, though, in the Northern Hemisphere give me north any day. Northward views are sunlit, glareless, and delightful. Looking to the north is like being at the movies. You look toward a brightly lighted scene from an area of relative darkness, the blinding light source behind you. (The view from south-facing windows is somewhat like the movies, too, except that all the seats have been reversed and you face the projector.)

Small Windows

It takes no great leap of logic to conclude that buildings should have large, south-facing windows for admitting sunlight and small north-facing windows for admitting views. The thought of having tiny windows, however, often seems oppressive, claustrophobic; but no one who's ever had the right kind has ever complained. It all depends on where you sit.

The most common of all tiny windows is the contact lens, followed closely by ordinary eyeglasses. Next come the windows of airplanes, cars, buses, and trains. America's most magnificent scenery is often viewed, without restriction, through both the small windows of one's spectacles and the small window of a vehicle. As I say, it all depends on where you sit. Obviously, one must sit close to a small window in order to have a large view.

People who live with great walls of glass all to often have nothing out there to look at anyway, and even the best views, made too easily available, lose some of their interest.

It's like all those pictures of naked, golden skin displayed on the magazine stands. Each month the pictures must show a little more in order to attract attention, but, back when only a few square inches of skin were shown, one's imagination had to be kept on a short leash simply to get one's self past all the printed wonders and on to the business of the day. Such is the attractiveness of the under-revealed.

Keyhole views, like gold and silver, are valued because of their limited supply. There's a window at Frank Lloyd Wright's famous Fallingwater House that must not be more than a foot or a foot and a half square, and yet it is the most memorable window in that partly glass house because the master arranged his spaces in such a way that the visitor is led to that window and made to appreciate the stunning view it frames. He didn't do this to save energy, but I see in it the potential joining of environmental priorities and really great architecture.

Part of the environmental side of that coming together is the proper insulation of windows, large and small. Windows alone, uninsulated, have a terrible reputation, thermally. It is a reputation well deserved.

Window Insulation

There are thought to be more than 2 billion windows in the United States, and every one is a heat waster, either letting heat in or letting heat out, just when it's supposed to stay put. Movable insulating shutters, either of the indoor or the outdoor type, if properly designed and installed and used, can reduce those heat losses dramatically, sometimes cutting fuel bills by as much as 50 percent. Being quite new, however, insulating shutters are still virtually unknown in America, but the sales potential of 2 billion windows, each one crying out for some sort of insulating device, has created a lot of interest and activity in the field.

The insulating shutters I've used have worked both fairly well (before I got the bugs out of the design), and very well (on later projects). I began by experimenting with the windows of my own building, making interior hinged panels of 1-in. urethane board in 1- by 3-in. frames, and covering the board with thin coats of fiberglass-reinforced plaster to give it a bit of fire resistance. Right away there were problems: warpage, poor fit, and limited room space; but the results of using the panels were little short of amazing. Our fuel bills dropped by more than 40 percent the first month.

Those first shutters were used at my Cherry Hill, New Jersey, office. Afterthoughts they were, added in reaction to my first winter there, the winter of 1971, when I learned that double glazing was not all one needed to prevent excessive heat losses through windows. The shutters never did fit very well; every temperature and humidity change warped them differently, making it difficult to readjust the foam-rubber air seals at the edges. Still, the heat losses dived, and the rooms became far more comfortable. Our body heat losses to the cold window wall were cut dramatically, too. We kept the shutters closed on every winter night, of course, and on weekends when we weren't working. We even kept most of the panels closed during the winter daytime when no sunlight was striking the glass. It's far cheaper to use a few small electric lights than it is to burn great quantities of fuel.

FIG. 6.1 *Interior hinged insulation panels of 1-in urethane in 1- by 2-in frames, and covered with 1/16-in fiberglass-reinforced plaster. Underground Office at Cherry Hill, N.J., 1970.* (Artog)

Hearing this, people often ask, "Do you mean to say that if you turned out all the lights on those sunless days when the shutters were closed, the rooms would have been pitch dark? Wasn't that a little depressing?" Ours wasn't an ideal installation, or course, but it was so much in tune with the weather and with the seasons, it became second nature to us to use the panels.

"You do them differently now, I take it."

"Yes. Now we often use translucent panels in order to admit more light."

Nowadays there are all kinds of devices available. It isn't necessary, any more, to create custom panels for each new installation. In addition to conventional storm windows and the ever-more-common taped-on-for-the-winter polyethylene sheets, there are inflatables, rolldownables, foldables, slideables, louver types, and beadwalls on the market. William Shurcliff has written an entire book about window-insulating and similar devices! *New Inventions in Low-Cost Solar Heating* (Brick House, 1979). A huge window-insulating industry seems to be waiting in the wings, ready to appear.

For individual small windows, you can't beat indoor, hinged shutters. They fold back out of the way, they're simple, trouble-free, and good-looking. But for large windows, I like sliding panels stacked at one side, each with an interlocking edge that links it to the next one. A floor space of about 10 by 24 inches will store the four panels needed to cover a standard 8-foot-wide patio slider. The important thing is to prevent air leaks through or around the panels, particularly at the sides and the bottoms. Trapped air gets very cold and heavy behind the closed panels, and it tries to leak into the room through every crack. The outdoor wind, pushing, as it inevitably does, through cracks around the window itself, helps push the icy, shutter-trapped air back into the room. It's conceivable, of course, that new discoveries and new glazing materials may make such devices as this obsolete. A new type of glass, said to be already fully developed, lets sunlight in but won't let much heat out. Even if that miracle comes to pass, there's still the problem of enormous heat losses around and through the window frames themselves. And, of course, the new miracle glass won't be cheap. To use it on America's two billion windows would mean a lot of glass replacement. My bet is that movable window insulating devices will be needed for at least a generation.

Doors

I spent a lot of time one year, back in the early sixties, and a lot of money, too, developing a door invention. It was a hole in the wall for doorknobs.

"Cavity Catch," I called it, and I actually hold a U.S. patent on the damned thing. According to the descriptive literature with which I tried to sell my idea to America's leading hardware manufacturers, not only could Cavity Catch save valuable inches of room and corridor space, but its hidden rubber friction button also helped keep the wind from slamming the doors. As in my earlier futile (and equally silly) campaigns against the window dressing of our environmental madness—billboards, overhead wires, and litter—I was still looking at superficial things, in this case at the surface qualities of doors, not at their door-y nature.

A door is a section of the wall mounted on hinges. Over the ages humanity in its infinite wisdom has seen fit to place the hinges at the side rather than at the top or the bottom of the door, and doors have become so much a part of our lives we hardly even see them anymore, let alone question our need for so many of them.

Doors, like windows, plywood, and much of our furniture, are rectangular because it's cheaper to manufacture and ship them that way, not because of the shapes of the things that pass through the openings to which the doors are hinged. Seen in that light, the idea of a person-shaped object passing through a rectangular doorway is ridiculous and awkward. A scaleless, rectangular hole punched through an architectural surface is often uncomfortable to behold. Doors should somehow be graceful parts of both the spaces and the walls to which they're related. It's all a question of appropriateness. When you think about aircraft design, it's quite obvious that most airplanes are good-looking, sometimes even beautiful, because they are purely functional. There are no frills, other than perhaps paint colors, on the outer surfaces of airplanes. They are built for function, not for style. Similarly, some of the big, long-distance trailer rigs—I'm talking about trucks—are good-looking because they express so well the idea of maximum cargo space passing within and through the confines of highway structures. A truck is exactly as high as the law allows it to be and exactly as wide. A truck is almost an extrusion. That's why trucks are so boxy and rectangular and getting ever more so. In trucks the rectangular shape make sense. In doors, sometimes it does not. All I ask is that doors not always be an unthinking 2½ feet wide and 6½ or 7 feet high—that doors and their openings by seen as powerful design elements.

The most important environmental thing that can be said about a door is the fact that indoors, in most cases, it is probably not even needed. Most interior doors are seldom if ever closed, and that alone represents a tremendous waste of building materials, space, and design potential, not to mention the lovely flowered wallpaper that's kept. hidden by all those always-open doors.

Exterior doors are often as guilty of heat leaking as windows are, and energy conservation devices like storm doors, vestibules, weatherstripping, and movable insulation are every bit as effective as their window counterparts.

Light

Total darkness is virtually unknown in our electrically lighted world, and many members of the TV generation have no concept at all of what honest-to-God nighttime is like. Raised in this age of floodlit, all-night shopping plazas, tens of millions of us have seldom seen any but the brightest of stars and have never known the sudden animallike alertness that comes from walking in inklike blackness on a cloudy night when nothing, no image at all, registers upon the retina. The act of walking under such conditions can be a very risky business indeed, a one-step-at-a-time testing of the path ahead, every footstep potential disaster, upraised arms crossed for protection in front of the face, ears more important than eyes, each sound sifted for a clue to the strange terrain. Under such conditions, all terrain, even the most familiar, is strange. It's more than daytime painted black; even the best-known route becomes a challenge. Reality assumes a different scale in the dark, and the night is full of little surprises. Walking in darkness is a good way to fall into an open trench, as a matter of fact, and it offers a chilling glimpse into the world of the newly blind. Walking in darkness reminds us of the twin miracles of a sunlit world and the eyes we need to see it.

When I walk at night on a country lane, and my eyes have adjusted to the softness of starlight, it's annoying, almost painful, to look at any man-made illumination. Country people are sometimes more annoyed by the light of a single floodlamp a mile away than the rest of us are by the multicolored glare that fills our nights. And rightly so: a lot more of the true spirit of nighttime gets destroyed by the country floodlight. There is no nighttime left to destroy along the strip.

One of my favorite routes for a country walk is almost free of artificial light. Only a single streetlamp interrupts the starlit peace. The interruption comes from an old-fashioned electric light, mounted on an ancient pole at an intersection. Compared to the newer mercury-vapor lamps, its light is the softest of the soft, and yet each time I round a certain bend and feel that far-ahead pin of brightness stab my nighttime eyes, it feels as if every one of its 400 watts is burning itself into my optic nerves—and that's when the lamppost is still a quarter mile away. As I move closer, it sometimes seems that all the light in the world is blazing there ahead of me, the contrast to the surrounding blackness is so great. Stars, trees, fields, fences—all disappear in what then becomes for a while a three-part world: the streetlight, my shadow, and me. If that lamp were lighted during the daytime, of course, even on the cloudiest of days, few people would even see it, its light is so weak compared to the light of day, but at night, with no daylight for competition, the brightness seems almost overwhelming. When I get to within 500 feet of it, I stop. I distract myself from the painful glare by remembering some mental calculations I once performed, there on that very spot. The line of reasoning went more or less like this:

Light radiates evenly in almost every direction from an ordinary lamp. No light, of course, can escape straight up the stem of the bulb, but as far as all other possible directions are concerned, the glowing surface of an incandescent lamp can be thought of as a simple sphere emitting radiation at an equal rate in all directions from each part of its evenly curved surface, each bit of radiance racing away at the speed of light, getting more diffuse with each foot of distance it travels from its source. Of all the light, then, that leaves the lamp, the amount that actually enters my eyes when I am 500 feet from it can be represented by that incredibly small part of a 1000-foot sphere encompassed by the area of my two night-dilated pupils. If each pupil is open to an aperture of ¼ inch under such light conditions, the combined surface area $(2\pi r^2)$ of the apertures is a mere tenth of a single square inch. Contrasted to that, the area $(4\pi r^2)$ of the imaginary 1000-foot sphere at the edge of which I stand is about 400 million square inches. Two simple calculations, two simple answers: One-tenth of a square inch for the area of my pupils, 400 million square inches for the area of the imaginary space-sphere upon which they lie. Two simple computations with a stunning message: The brightness that so annoys me on my favorite country walk is actually so small a part—only one 4-billionth—of that streetlight's total radiation, that *all the people on earth,* all 4 billion of us, could be equally and simultaneously annoyed by the power of its 400-watts: Even standing eyeball-to-eyeball, of course, there's no way all the people on earth could squeeze close enough to merge their pupils into a continuous window on that giant, imaginary 1000-foot sphere, but the numbers illustrate my point nonetheless.

Let me run through all that again. Two tiny windows in the front of my head admit enough of the light from a block-distant streetlamp to cause discomfort, if not outright pain, in spite of the fact that they admit less than one 4-billionth part of all the light radiated from the bulb. Of the lamp's total 400-watt output, only one 10-millionth of a watt's-worth ever reaches my retinas, yet somehow that light, under those conditions, still seems too bright. How's that for sensitivity?

In adjusting itself from full-aperture nighttime vision (in which even one

4-billionth part of the light from a common streetlamp can be annoying) to the daytime, high-glare, beach-haze brightness near the other end of my optic scale, my eye spans an intensity range almost beyond comprehension. And when I remember that my tiny share of light received from that lonely rural lamp is still enough to obscure most stars, the versatility of the human eye goes altogether beyond my understanding.

Bringing this down to even more familiar terms, when I sit at a table in the light of a 100-watt lamp, up close, my actual eyeshare of the total radiation is still quite small. Paraphrasing the streetlight calculations: of all the light that leaves the lamp, the amount that actually enters my eyes when I am 3 feet from it can be represented by that tiny part of a 6-foot sphere encompassed by the area of my two light-shrunk pupils. If the diameters of those apertures have been reduced by the intense brightness to ⅛ inch, the combined surface area $(2\pi r^2)$ of the apertures is a mere fortieth part of a single square inch. Contrasted to that, the area $(4\pi r^2)$ of the imaginary 6-foot sphere at the edge of which I sit is about 16,000 square inches. Two simple calculations, two simple answers: One fortieth part of a square inch for the area of my pupils, 16,000 square inches for the area of the imaginary space-sphere upon which they lie. Two simple calculations with another stunning message: At most *only one 600,000th part of that 100-watt glow ever enters my eyes.* If no one shares that light with me, all 599,999 other parts go wasted. In order for the eyes to use even 1 percent of the total output of a 100-watt lamp, they'd have to be inside the light bulb itself, within a half inch of the glowing filament!

So the science of energy conservation, at least with respect to illumination technology, has barely been born; far more than 99 percent of all the light produced on earth is never seen at all.

I have traveled by air from Philadelphia to Los Angeles on two occasions, arriving, both times, at night, and, both times, I've heard an involuntary gasp fill the cabin as the lights of the city appeared. As far as the eye could see, strings of colored lights, uncountable millions of them, jeweled the blackened plain. Regardless of one's energy opinions, the night view of Los Angeles has got to be one of the more impressive sights on earth.

But it's not necessary to go to California for such a show. Barnesville, Ohio, or Goober, Alabama, seen from the air at night, is enough to make anyone gasp. The point is that we're flinging a lot of hard-won energy away into space each night, the light spectacle being but the visible part, the iceberg tip, of our total energy loss. The loss from outdoor lighting alone must be staggering. Without even considering the ratio of total light to that tiny part which actually enters the human eye, but considering only the ratio of total light output to that part which actually illuminates a subject, the energy waste is still phenomenal. Every particle of light seen from the window of an airplane, or from a nearby hill, or from the house next door, is *total waste* — energy lost forever to all possibility of human use. We lose more that way each year, and we respond to that loss by generating more electricity, drawing ourselves closer and closer to total dependence upon the most frightening power source of all, the nuclear one. If we did it with evil intent, we'd be a race of monsters, and there are those who can weave a convincing case for that view of mankind. But it seems to me we aren't guilty at all, that we are at worst simply uninformed, the products of misguided educations. Even our teachers knew no better. The change from simple and relatively harmless use of the earth to our complicated and deadly use of it was so gradual that few people even noticed it until lately.

They say it takes about a tenth of a second from the time an oncoming car appears for a motorist to begin to apply the brakes. The lag is called reaction time. It is a factor that must be considered in the timing of every response to a stimulus. When the entire race has to put on the brakes, its reaction time becomes somewhat longer than a tenth of a second. Most of us haven't even sensed the possibility of an accident; many of us have seen something ahead, but can't tell, just yet, if it will be a blessing or a curse; and some of us have seen nothing unusual at all. Until a majority of us can agree on what it is that looms out there in front of us, we can hardly be expected to take effective countermeasures. Whether or not an agreement can be reached before something very spectacular happens in our little corner of the universe is anyone's guess, but in any case it's going to take us a long, long time to see, to decide, and then to act.

Having had wide experience in creating energy waste of all kinds during the earlier years of my practice, I am perhaps in a somewhat better position than most people to appreciate the extent of the threat we face. But even today, with energy conservation as one of my major interests, I continue to produce buildings that waste light and other forms of energy. Part of the waste is attributable to my still far-from-complete understanding of the subject, part is from science's own shortcomings in that regard, part is from a lack of efficient lighting devices, and part is from the human element at work in the construction industry. The power companies, of course, would like us all to go on as before, leaving to them all decisions as to what is best for us. But our occasional glimpses into the workings of the public utilities show us that people no smarter than we are confidently go about making the most frightening kinds of decisions. We've got to take the matter out of their hands by taking the only course that's certain to be safe — conservation. And conservation, like almost everything else, must begin at home. The American family uses huge amounts of electrical energy. Most of it goes for heating purposes of various kinds: space heating, water heating, clothes drying, cooking— that sort of thing; and heating is the worst possible use of electricity. But the subject at hand is lighting, and light, like smoke and litter, is a visible expression of our energy waste. It can help us see that we're doing something wrong.

Noise

Noise, on the other hand, can help us *hear* that we're doing something wrong, and there's plenty of such evidence afloat on the nervous American air. I am told that, to the sightless, every space—indoor, outdoor, large, and small—has a quality few of us sighted persons can even imagine. Based on acoustics alone, space reveals its true, three-dimensional quality. Sounds come to us from all directions, not just from the front— the way most sight perceptions come—but also from above, behind, and below, at every conceivable angle. Some sounds move directly from source to ear, but most come bouncing toward us from nearby surfaces, adding both richness and confusion to the reception. Some sound sources move, some are fixed; and the bounced, or reflected, sounds carry with them clues to the qualities of the surfaces from which they ricochet. All the sounds being received by the ear at any given moment, if undifferentiated, become simply noise. Separated, perceived one by one, they offer telltale clues to our surroundings.

When you close your eyes and concentrate on what your ears are receiving, you will be surprised at first by the ugliness of the noise to which most of us are constantly exposed. Then, as its components are identified, you can catch a glimpse, so to speak, of the space world all sightless persons inhabit. Even without practice it's possible to hear great numbers of different sounds within the general noise. Not long ago, in the waiting room of the Barnstable County Airport in Hyannis, I decided to test this idea. To my great surprise I found that I was able to identify dozens of separate sounds in just a few minutes.

Each sound told me something. Its first message was, or at least should have been, the fact that energy was being expended. When all forces are at rest, silence results. It's hard to believe that even in the noisiest room, the sounds of watches ticking, breaths being breathed, and pens moving on paper are still adding their little vibrations to the quivering air. It is, of course, only the practiced ear which can discern them in the greater confusion, and it is a rare ear indeed that can pick from among all the sounds those which actually describe and measure the space around it. Total silence, in this world of living creatures, of natural forces, and of man and his noise binge is, if you will excuse the expression, almost unheard of. Only in a carefully constructed anechoic chamber can anything approaching total silence be perceived, and the experience is so unfamiliar it's disconcerting, sometimes disorienting and terrifying. Somewhere between total silence and the chaotic jangle most of us endure there is a level of noise, of sounds, that is both pleasant and rewarding. Gentle architecture has this quality as its acoustic goal.

At the airport I mentioned, I found it interesting not only to identify each sound component of the general noise but also to think about what each component had to tell me. Listing those airport sounds in five sections may help make the uproar less confusing. I found that by listening, in turn, only for the sounds of each category I was able to shut out all other sounds until I was ready for them.

Sounds produced by mechanical and electrical devices:
Public address announcements. Poorly reproduced, too loud, and with annoying reverberations.

Tearoom-type music played continuously. Very poor selections, poor renditions, poor reproduction, annoying reverberations.

Telephones ringing.

Air system noise, mostly a whistling "whoosh" at the poorly designed air grilles, but it included the distant thrumming sound of a fan.

Electric typewriter.

Teletype printer.

Compressor cycling on and off to chill the water at a drinking fountain.

Toilets being flushed. (Think about the water waste, and where all the sewage is going!)

Motors running somewhere. (Where is there not a motor to be heard somewhere in the distance?)

Aircraft taking off.

Change being returned at a pay telephone.

Sound produced by nonliving natural forces:
Wind whistling at an exit door during gusts.

Ticking, probably of expansion or contraction in the building structure.

Sounds produced by the actions of living creatures:
Thump of a validation stamping machine at a check-in counter.

Footsteps—many kinds—on the hard floor surfaces.

Slam of a door.

Clink and clatter at the luncheonette counter.

Rustle of newspapers and magazines.

Plop of a heavy, unfit body dropping gracelessly into a seat.

Tap on an ashtray as a janitor empties waste receptacles.

Footsteps on carpet.

Telephone receiver being dropped back onto its cradle.

Snap of plastic time-and-destination cards being changed at the flight-announcement board.

Rustle of my clothing.

Click of my pen tapping against my tooth.

Strike of a match.

Ding as it hits the ashtray.

Sounds of living creatures other than myself:
Harsh, penetrating laugh.

An unpleasant voice.

Shrieks of recognition and greeting.

Many voices at various distances.

Coughs.

Sneezes.

Grunt of a heavy, unfit body dropping gracelessly into a seat.

Breathing (labored).

Clearing of throats.

Barking of a dog (distant).

Crying of a baby.

Sounds of my own body:
Squishing of saliva. (Surprisingly noisy! Try it.)

Swallowing. (Also noisier than I'd ever noticed.)

Clicking together of teeth that usually accompanies swallowing.

Breathing.

Scratching of my scalp.

A faint ringing in one ear. (Probably not a true sound.)

The ear is a marvelous thing, marvelous not only in what it can detect but also in what it can tolerate. A jet engine operating at close range is some *ten thousand* times as loud as the sound of rustling leaves. No wonder "deafening" noises are so painful. Even though the sounds of the wilderness in which we evolved are almost always in the "faint" or "very quiet" ranges, engineers, architects, and designers of sound equipment routinely specify noise levels *20 or 30 times as high* for spaces in which human beings must live and work! No wonder we have high blood pressure. It's directly related, at least in part, to the noise levels around us.

Are you familiar with the term "decibel" by which loudness levels are specified? The range, for the human ear, from the soft rustling of leaves to deafening explosions, is from about 10 on the decibel scale to 150—not a very impressive-looking span, almost like the normal outdoor range of a fahrenheit thermometer. But decibel numbers alone are misleading. On the thermometer the upward progression is linear; 20 degrees are as much warmer than 10 degrees as 30 are warmer than 20. That's not the case with decibels. On the decibel scale a noise rated at 20 is *ten times* as loud as one at 10, and 30 is ten times more than 20! The actual scale is as follows:

Decibels	Factor
0	1
10	10
20	100
30	1,000
40	10,000
50	100,000
60	1,000,000
70	10,000,000
80	100,000,000
90	1,000,000,000
100	10,000,000,000
110	100,000,000,000
120	1,000,000,000,000
130	10,000,000,000,000
140	100,000,000,000,000
150	1,000,000,000,000,000

We live submerged in a world far noisier than our ears or nerves were designed to handle, and, for some of us, there is literally no escape. How can anyone say this is not an architectural problem? Granted, it may seem wrong to accommodate an environmental mistake (noise) by creating silent refuges from it, but what else are we to do?

Gentle architecture offers refuge from noise. Not only do more natural buildings dispense with many of the machines which produce it, they also damp, and sometimes even eliminate, noise from other sources. I've visited anechoic chambers, those acoustic-laboratory vaults in which almost no sound exists, and I know them to be somewhat frightening. The *absence* of all noise—or sound—seems almost to exert a pressure on the ears. But I have also spent a lot of time in underground buildings, which are not frightening because there are always tiny, if unnoticed, reverberations present, and I have enjoyed those escapes from our noisy world. In the little north toilet room of my former office building in New Jersey, which was only 18 feet from the edge of a booming six-lane highway, I could stand absolutely still and hear nothing but the sounds of my own breathing and the just barely audible sound of a 50-year-old heart. When I swallowed, of course, it was like cymbals and drums, and I wanted to cheer at all the excitement.

Solar Greenhouses

Greenhouses, sometimes known as glasshouses or hothouses, are used for extending local growing seasons or for creating year-round plant environments for species foreign to a particular area. Until the 1973 Arab oil embargo, America and many other countries were undergoing a greenhouse-building boom. Premium prices for fresh-cut flowers and winter vegetables spurred commercial greenhouse growth, and the fun and prestige of having one's own garden room at home was boosting the consumer market as well. But it all came to a screeching, if temporary, halt when oil prices rose, for greenhouses are perhaps first among building types when it comes to fuel use.

The energy crisis, as that pimple on the real crisis came to be called, helped push both amateur and professional greenhouse users to more efficient management of their glassy fuel wasters and sparked the development of more appropriate designs. It also popularized the idea of the *solar* greenhouse, a name that at first seems redundant but which looks extremely appealing once one sees how unsolar traditional greenhouses have been.

A solar greenhouse is one in which all, or most, of the heat and light necessary for plant growth comes from the sun. Ideally, a solar greenhouse will produce even more heat than it needs, in which case the excess can be used by the building to which it is attached. This development has already become so popular that the greenhouse boom is on again, this time with less undesirable environmental consequences.

I've designed many solar greenhouses but such is the lack of speed at which buildings move from drawing boards to construction that I have, as yet, not one completed glass structure to my credit. Maybe I'm lucky; so much new information is coming out so continuously it's probably just as well that I learn a bit more while I wait. But even with what is known about them today, solar greenhouses are highly practical, and they can be built for very little money, sometimes paying for themselves with the food-cost savings of a single year.

Irwin Spetgang, Saburo Takama, and I designed a special greenhouse at the request of a Swedish group interested in the development of sub-arctic areas. The design involved the use of huge, movable, mirrored insulation lids to catch the low-angle winter sunlight of the region, and to shut, sealing in the spaces during the long, dark nights, at which time solar energy in another form, wind energy, was to have powered banks of growth lights. The project was shelved.

Another greenhouse was the one designed for the Locust Hill House at Raven Rocks in Ohio. There, all the solar work was developed by

Total Environmental Action* (TEA) and the Raven Rocks people, but I was the one who integrated them with the rest of the structure. The Raven Rocks greenhouses are now under construction.

Another greenhouse is to be attached to the laboratory at the Plant Science Building of the Cary Arboretum. The Arboretum already has large conventional greenhouses which it has altered in such ways as to produce dramatic fuel savings, but they are not truly solar greenhouses. This little design, which borrows heavily from pioneering work done by many others in the field, is shaped to comply with the 30° to 60° geometry of the other parts of the building, and it appears that these angles will work out very well (see Chapter 8). The keys to greenhouse success: thermal mass to store the excess sun energy; and insulation, both fixed and movable.

FIG. 6.2

Gray Water

Another key to greenhouse success can be gray water. It's the name given to that portion of sewage, most often household sewage, which contains no human wastes. It can consist of sink, tub, laundry, or shower water. I've had no direct experience with it, myself, but I've seen a lot of promising installations—treatment ponds, greenhouses, composting beds. These prove to me, beyond a doubt, that far better ways are ready and waiting for us than those we use in our buildings today. So far, all I've done is to separate gray and human waste pipes until they reach some convenient point—inside a basement or just outside a foundation wall. Then I join the pipes and use whatever method of sewage disposal seems most appropriate under the circumstances. The point of having the two lines, of course, is that by keeping the two kinds of wastes separate, the gray water line can be quite easily directed to a separate treatment system or to a greenhouse, or to whatever else of promise comes along.

Abby Rockefeller, who handles the Clivus Multrum system† in the

*TEA's address: Church Hill, Harrisville, NH 03450.
†The best knwon of the Clivus Multrum products is a waterless, sewerless composting device which replaces conventional human waste and kitchen waste systems. For information write to 17A Eliot St., Cambridge, MA 02131.

United States, has, in an experimental greenhouse, a system which not only uses gray water to feed and irrigate the plants, it also cleans the waste-bearing water by natural filtration and decomposition processes. In other buildings, where large quantities of gray water are produced, the warmth of the water itself is sometimes used in heating other water, or in heating the buildings. There are many variations on the gray water idea, all of which are better than what 99 percent of us are still doing: polluting streams or ground water with our water-borne wastes. The main thing, the first step, is to keep human wastes and gray-water wastes separate. Without that first step, there's little hope of doing anything worthwhile with either component.

As we learn more about greenhouses—solar-heated greenhouses in particular—we'll automatically be moving ourselves closer to the time when all of us, not just the greenhouse or the gray-water experts, can combine the product of our metabolic processes into integrated biological soil enrichment and food production systems.

Some of the qualities of soils, of this granular stuff beneath our feet, are listed below, and anyone more than superficially interested in using the earth more wisely in conjunction with architecture would be well advised to do some research in these matters.

Soils

Weight of various soils
Specific heat of various soils
Thermoconductivity of various soils
Nature and properties of soils
Fundamentals of soil science
Chemical properties of forest soils
Soil conditions and plant growth
Influence of vegetation on soil temperatures
Geology of soils
Conductance of soils
Resistivity of various soils.

As you can see, there's far too much involved to allow easy generalizations. What we call soil—common, ordinary dirt—seems to be as complicated as we are. But there is one earth fact worth mentioning here. Too many of us still believe that earth is a good insulator; too many of us assume that by burying a building in the earth it is in that way well protected, thermally. It is not. For instance, an inch of average dry soil has a thermal resistivity, that is, an R factor, of 0.39. An inch of urethane board has an R factor of 7.0. That's about 18 times as good as earth. The great value of surrounding buildings with earth is not so much one of insulation, but of the slowing down of temperature changes. It takes a long time for that great earth mass to change temperatures, and that slowing down, that flywheel effect, used in combination with a conventional insulation material of some type, really works wonders.

Earth's other thermal and energy-saving advantages are that, even though the temperature of the soil on a rooftop may slowly drop to the freezing level or below, it is still far warmer than the frigid air that chilled it. The other advantage: the end of all wind-losses. Much is made of the windchill factor. It robs both bodies and buildings of their heat far faster when the air round them is moving. The fastest wind ever clocked underground didn't even register on the scale, so slow was the breeze.

Radiation

In the soil no radioactive particles blow, either, and yet I hesitate—I hate—to mention the radiation-shielding advantages of earth-covered buildings. Anything that makes the threat of nuclear war or a nuclear accident even the slightest bit more tolerable seems to be terribly regressive. I know that the Chinese, and the Russians, are building vast underground facilities, and that there may well come a day on which an historian, looking back upon this age, will see that only the Russians and the Chinese survived it, their judgment having in that way been proved correct. Maybe. But the thought of building underground for that purpose seems not only to make war more acceptable, it seems to me cowardly as well. Here's what I mean: if we're going to build underground structures for that purpose, then *the creatures to be sheltered there should not be human ones,* at least not the combatants.

It is to all the legions of the uninvolved, to the Third World, that we owe such protection. They, and the even more uninvolved *natural* creatures of the world, are the ones a fair-minded race would want to defend. What kind of sportsmanship is it to create a nuclear threat and then protect only ourselves from it, letting all the innocent parties roast?

Imported Resources

We should not only be concerned about the innocent and the uninvolved, we should also care about the resources we squander. We're not as independent as we sometimes think. A great number of the natural resources most vital to this country come from beyond our borders. The

U.S. Bureau of Mines has published a list of them. It's shown in the form of a graph, below. What the Bureau didn't publish when it produced the figures on the graphs were statistics on the amount of energy—fuel—needed to ship all those resources here, let alone to move them through all the subsequent fabrication, assembly, packaging and transport operations. Nor was there any mention of the way we waste so much of what we use. I suspect that those statistics would be the most shocking of all.

This is another subject they forgot to teach us at architectural school, one that has huge political, military, environmental, and, of course, architectural ramifications. Every line you draw and every specification you write affects, and is affected by, what you see on this graph.

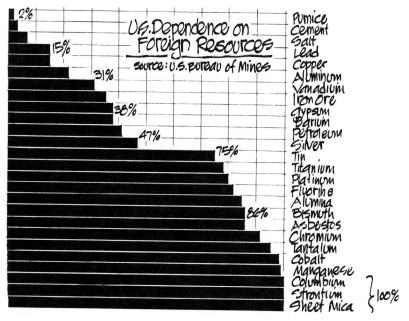

FIG. 6.3

CHAPTER SEVEN

Materials

Concrete

According to the April 1978 issue of *Progressive Architecture,* Americans use 450,000,000 cubic yards* of concrete every year. That's over 6000 pounds of concrete annually for every man, woman, and child in the nation. What we're doing with it all I can't imagine. What it all costs in terms of energy must be staggering.

Here is what Warren Stetzel had to say after I asked him how much energy goes into the making and delivering of a yard of concrete:

> Thinking about the matter makes one realize what a complex business that kind of calculation is going to be. Do you go all the way back on all the route lines, what it took to manufacture the truck and the fuel as well as the cement itself? Or the processing of the sand and gravel, their transportation, and so on? Is the concrete type 1, or type 1T? Type 1T cuts energy use 20 percent per bag of cement unless you count the energy invested in the fly ash that was used to make the special cement. But do you do that, or assign that to the production of electricity or styrene? A polymer company that produces plastics in Pennsylvania produces 80 tons of fly ash per day in just one of its factories.

There seem to be no generally accepted figures on how much energy actually goes into the production of a yard of concrete, and yet here we are, architects and engineers in the lead, using over a million cubic yards of it every day.

What many people call cement, we architects call concrete. It is an artificial, sandy limestone, and it has all the strength of the real thing. Imagine having stone you can pour! It must be one of the most useful materials known to man. Used for the construction of roads, walks, plazas, bridges, dams, foundations, and buildings, it may at some future time become the principal material by which archaeologists are able to recognize our era, for concrete is sometimes very long lasting. The trouble with concrete is that you've first got to build an entire structure of wood or metal, called a form, to pour it into. Then you have to tear down that

---

*A single cubic yard of concrete weighs 3050 pounds.

giant mold, piece by piece, and try to use as much of it as possible over again in order to save money. And the trouble with formwork is that, since we are not by nature a careful people, its potential for reuse and its actual reuse are quite different. We don't deal with the matter by taking proper care of the forms. Instead, characteristically, we adopt a high-tech solution: we *precast* the concrete in a factory, then truck it to the site, there to have it put together like the pieces of a giant Erector Set.

Precasting has given us some very handsome structures, most of which are quite strong, and some of which were built at surprisingly low cost. Factory-built components offer degrees of economy and quality control that are impossible to match in the field. But I wonder if that's really the appropriate way to handle such a plastic material, one that so beautifully flows into place on the site, making the building almost a stony extension of the earth itself. When I picture precast (versus poured-in-place) concrete being used for a building on or in the earth, I see something like a precast filling being forced into a tooth. The picture is unfair but then I've made no claim to being a fair person.

Because of its pourability, concrete can be molded into all kinds of shapes, and if you do everything right it will hold those shapes for decades, even for centuries. If you do enough wrong, of course, you may find that several tons of caustic mud that were poured only a few moments earlier into roof-level forms are now quickly turning to stone down in the basement. Or, even when the forms support their wet load adequately, as most forms do, the architect may find great chunks of his aerial masterpiece cracking loose after the first hard freeze. It can't be fooled with, concrete; you have to follow most of the rules.

Like its authentic counterpart, stone, plain concrete can support great weight, but it can carry it only in direct compression, not when the load tends to stretch or bend it. That's why most concrete gets reinforced, why we embed steel bars in it. Like sinews, they help overcome the deficiencies inherent in plain, unreinforced concrete.

It is often useful, when thinking about the structural qualities of concrete, to imagine it as being comprised of lightly glued, flat stones stacked to the size of the total mass, rather than as a single monolithic object. Obviously, such stacks of stones could support great weight if it were applied only from above, straight down. Once you turned them on their sides to create a beam, they'd be doing well just to support their own weight, so weak is their gluing, and, as this flat-stones analogy implies, it would be even worse if you tried to exert a stretching force upon them. By picturing plain concrete in this way, you can often see at a glance things many structural books take pages to prove. You can almost feel the stresses acting upon the material, and you can see what it is that

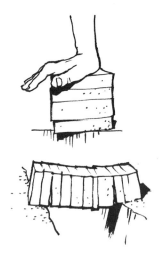

FIG. 7.1

reinforcing bars do to improve its performance. They work in harmony with those imaginary slabs within its mass to resist the forces of bending, pulling, slipping, and bursting. Steel holds the concrete together, and the concrete, using its compressive strength to carry the direct loads, keeps the bars from getting out of alignment or buckling. Sometimes, of course, no matter how well a beam or slab is reinforced, it just isn't up to the job. Thin horizontal slabs or beams too long for their depth will begin to sag in response to the ever-present vibrations of the modern world and to the endless tug of gravity. If concrete hasn't been used right, a whole bookful of untoward consequences can come into play.

Concrete's strength is so dependent upon so many things it seems a wonder sometimes that concrete ever stands up at all. That's why we have, and need, tough building codes with plenty of safety factors in them. The basic materials of which concrete is made are sand and stone and powdered cement. When water is added the cement begins to crystallize, locking the sand and gravel (and any reinforcing bars) into place. If the materials are wrongly proportioned (too little cement, or too much water or sand), or there is too long a delay, or improper mixing, or careless placing, or inadequate curing, or any of a dozen other mistakes, the concrete will turn out to have far less strength than it was intended to have, and the emerging structure will begin to feel very unhappy. If the steel bars are too rusty or oily, the cement won't stick to them. They will be almost useless. If they are of the wrong size or strength, or if they are put in the wrong places, again they will be almost useless. It's a tricky business, one that few architects or builders fully understand. But will we admit it? Not too often.

Most of us architects are interested in both the strength and the finish, the surface, of the concrete. Builders tend to be more concerned with the workability, the wetness, of the mix and with construction costs—with whether or not the cement finisher will have to work overtime and other such matters. They have secret ways of speeding or retarding the setting-up of fresh concrete with an eye to the payroll. All of these maneuvers affect the eventual result which usually comes up somewhere within the limits of acceptability, but a long, long way from the kind of concrete that might have been. Still, very few concrete buildings ever fall down, and we must remember, now and then, to be very grateful for that.

Unlike mud, concrete does not get hard simply because it gets dry. In fact, it need never get dry at all in order to harden, or set. Everyone seems to have heard about concrete being poured successfully under water. Still, most of us tend to associate concrete's liquid-to-solid change with the act of drying. The phenomenon of a muddy, gray slurry turning almost rock hard in a few hours is a process many architects, I among them, find endlessly fascinating, almost addictive. After all, how many other people in this world ever have a chance to see the lines they've drawn on paper turn into huge masses of molded stone?

The setting, or hardening, of concrete is a process that generates considerable heat. It goes on with great speed for a few hours, then continues at an ever-slower rate for days, weeks, months, and years, a fact to which anyone who has tried to chisel away a bit of old concrete can attest. To avoid excessively diluting the magic of crystallization, the mix should be prepared with the minimum quantity of water necessary to provide uniform dispersion of the ingredients and then to keep the new concrete moist for a week or so in order to prevent premature drying, which, if it occurs, will interfere with the proper hardening of the cement. Because of the heat generated by the concrete itself, drying often occurs faster than one would tend to have guessed, considering the gallons and gallons of water used in every yard of even the driest concrete. That's why the curing of the material has to be watched as carefully as the pouring, and why the control of concrete quality consumes such a big part of the time spent by all the hard-hatted men with clipboards you see at most construction sites. Concrete designers insist on low-water mixes, placed with great care, followed by several days of constant wetting, but the people actually doing the work quietly try to water-down the still-liquid mix for easy pouring, and then do as little additional watering as possible after the concrete has been placed and given an acceptable finish.

Some familiar excuses heard during the pouring process: *"What* hose? Oh, I didn't know it was running." Or, "I thought you wanted it this way." Or, "It's not as wet as it looks—feel it." Or, "How do you expect us to work with dry concrete?" And later, during the curing period: "I can't understand what happened. I told them to keep that stuff wet." Those are the times at which the architect or the structural engineer has golden opportunities to show off his skills as both diplomat and tyrant. It's almost a no-win situation, of course. The guy with the trowel in his hand is absolutely free of liability in the claims which may grow out of his negligence. He'll sleep soundly that night, and he knows it. The architect, the structural engineer, the contractor, and even the owner, however, are always open to costly and time-consuming legal battles over any deficiencies in the structure. That's why design professionals have to carry—and try to pass on to their clients the cost of—ever-more-expensive professional liability insurance, and why they are writing ever-stricter specifications and recording every significant decision made on the job. The cover-your-butt syndrome has generated so much documentation there's almost as much paper involved in a yard of concrete as there is cement. But it's either that or the possibility of having to pay some heavy claims.

Concrete is sometimes advertised as being inherently waterproof, and many additives are available to increase its water-retarding qualities, but, except for the samples demonstrated by the building materials salesmen, I have never seen a concrete that I would be willing to call waterproof. Concrete alone cannot resist leakage because it cannot seal its own cracks, and concrete is very good at cracking. If it is improperly designed or constructed, of course, concrete can develop very large cracks, their causes ranging from such things as structural design errors, too-fast drying, and premature or excessive loading, to failure to provide expansion or control joints and disturbance of the material during setting. But even when everything has been done correctly, the development of hairline cracks in concrete seems to be almost inevitable, and none of them are too narrow to admit water. That's why it's best to apply waterproofing (to the outer surface, to the weather or earth side) rather than rely solely upon an easily cracked material that's so vulnerable to the effects of mishandling in the field.

To get both high strength and a good surface finish, you need the services of a concrete construction expert. He uses all the best practices and makes good use of mechanical vibrators, those motorized rods that make the semisolid material flow into all the corners of the forms and around every bar of steel. But even that is at best an imperfect art. In the finest of concrete buildings you can usually find places the vibrator didn't reach—often at the bottoms of columns or walls, where a telltale condition called honeycombing appears. Honeycombing is hated by structural engineers and by most architects, but I happen to love the look of it.

FIG. 7.2 *Detail of honeycombing in wall at original Cherry Hill office, 1965.*

Most "good" concrete surfaces are so smooth they have no character. They might as well be made of plain, gray wallpaper. The evidence of trapped air bubbles on the concrete surfaces adds a bit of interest to the effect, but it is the honeycombing in the wall that gives the material the rugged look of honest-to-God concrete. The only trouble is that honeycombing can indicate a serious structural defect. Obviously, if spaces remain around some of the pebbles in the mix, they can't be fully cemented together. Sometimes a honeycombed portion is so weak it can be knocked out of the wall with one good kick, scattering pebbles in all directions. That's when the designer of the concrete is faced with a tough question: What to do? Condemn the entire wall and demand its replacement, or simply patch the weakened part? Luckily, there are accepted criteria available for such job crises, and it is the wise designer or contractor who follows them carefully.

Honeycombing really is bad news, and yet I know of one instance in which it defied all the rules. My first office once stood in the center of an open, grassy acre. Then, one day, the State Highway Department decided it was time to widen a nearby boulevard to within 10 feet of the building wall, and soon six lanes of roaring car and truck traffic were speeding by, within spitting distance of my drawing board. So I designed a wall, a great wall of concrete, 50 feet long and 10 feet high. It was very easy to draw, but the only contractor who didn't want an arm and a leg to build it had had very little concrete experience. But then, so, too, had I. He'd done plenty of 50-foot-long concrete jobs before, but they had all been of the basement floor variety—50 feet long, and 4 inches (not 10 feet) high. Still, he set about the work with confidence, building the forms twice as strong as was necessary in order not to generate any muddy surprises for the trucks and buses whizzing by only an arm's length away. But he had never heard about vibrators. He just dumped the concrete into the forms and let it do what it wanted. He'd spout a few tons at one point until they were level with the top, then he'd signal the driver of the ready-mix truck to move a few feet farther along the wall and repeat the process. The wall was poured in no time. A few days later, when the contractor removed the forms, he found to his very great embarrassment and to my surprise that I had bought, for years to come, a perfect expression, wrought in artificial stone, of his whole amateurish procedure. I hadn't seen waves that far from an ocean in my entire life.

The real surprise, however, was that they were beautiful. They were almost as appealing as the wild swirls of color exposed in some of the natural rock walls along highway cuts. The honeycomb patterns were musically graceful, and, after we'd done some planting, landscaping made them even better. But most people, on seeing the wall, told me it

FIG. 7.3 *Honeycombed wall at original Cherry Hill office, 1965.*

FIG. 7.4 *Highway cut, New York State*

would never survive a winter. "Why, the ice will get into all those little crevices and bust that wall wide open." "There's not enough cement left between those pebbles to hold up for a month with all the truck vibrations you get here."

That was in 1964, and now, half a generation later, after being shaken by millions of cars, a minor earthquake, and a couple of sonic booms, the wall is almost as solid as ever. Only a few handfuls of pebbles have been dislodged. It has withstood searing summers and record winters, ice storms and hail, downpours and windstorms. And its lesson?

I'm not sure. I'd never advise anyone else to build that way, and I've grown so cautious, now, I wouldn't even try to do it again myself, but I love that old wall in Cherry Hill, New Jersey, and I make a point of inspecting it whenever I return to that area. Maybe the water drains so quickly out of all the crevices there is never a chance for any ice damage to occur. Or maybe it was just beginner's luck. I don't know. Whatever it was, it turned out really well, and I wish that somehow all concrete could safely have a bit of that wall's rich texture. It's another reason why I enforce the low-water content requirement of the concrete specifications, and why I never insist on excessive vibration. There's always a chance that a nice band of honeycombing (of the harmless, surface type) will occur as a result.

In addition to its strength and beauty, concrete has another quality called *thermal mass*. It's the property of concrete and other heavy materials to store considerable amounts of heat for use later on. Traditionally, the outer surfaces of concrete buildings were left exposed to the weather. Their insulation, if any, was placed on the inner surfaces of the outer walls. Now we know that such buildings can be far, far more efficient if their insulation is placed on the *outer* surface of the concrete, so that the great mass of the material itself can store extra heat energy within the insulation envelope and help stabilize otherwise fluctuating interior temperatures. In such applications proper thermal detailing is extremely important, and no indoor-outdoor material can be allowed. Thermal breaks—insulation—must be used between the indoor concrete and any concrete left exposed to the cold if an energy bleed is to be avoided.

There are a lot of tricks involved in getting heat to penetrate deep into concrete. It neither absorbs nor releases energy very quickly. But if those tricks are followed, if air or water is passed through it by means of pipes or ducts, or through corrugations in or under the concrete, great amounts of heat can be stored there and then withdrawn when needed later on.

Concrete should not be used just for its thermal mass, of course. A lot of other materials—water being by far the best—can do the job for a lot less money. Only when concrete is right, structurally, should its thermal character be exploited as well.

Another property of concrete now coming to be appreciated more and more is its humidity-blotting power. Concrete is an effective stabilizer of room moisture.

In our rush to escape the noise and wastefulness of machinery, we have turned sometimes too quickly to passive kinds of architecture that bring us other kinds of problems. One, particularly in tightly sealed buildings, is that of excessive humidity—dampness, mildew, moisture—and we're finding that concrete, like brick and stone, particularly when sealed on its outside (earth-retaining) surface and exposed to the room, goes a long way toward combating those conditions. When concrete walls and columns and beams have been externally waterproofed they will actually absorb huge amounts of water vapor from room air, helping to stabilize its relative humidity. This is a quality that tanks of water, while far better storers of heat, do not have. Concrete's moisture-holding properties are particularly helpful in underground buildings where the tendency toward dampness is always present. (I'm not talking about leaks.) Both above and below ground, if a building's walls are cool, and warm, humid air is allowed to come in contact with them, the air will try to dump its load of moisture on the cool surfaces. By admitting plenty of sunlight deep into the building, by circulating—mixing—the air, and by insulating the walls so that they're not quite so cool, much of the tendency toward condensation and dampness can be overcome. Still, there is the problem, particularly in the summertime, of damp air causing unpleasant conditions. That's when this blotting power of concrete walls comes into play. It can actually make the difference between a pleasant environment and a very unhealthful and musty one.

I know of a concrete house, a concrete *underground* house, near a pond, near a seashore, in an area where fogs and dampness are often present. It's so damp there, in fact, that the pines have mossy beards growing from their branches. The house is left open all summer, and yet for some reason no dampness is evident. Why? The only explanation I can find for the phenomenon is that the massive concrete walls soak up this excess moisture when the air is wet, hold it for as long as necessary, and then release it to the atmosphere when the air is dry.

As you can see, I think concrete is a pretty nice material. Imagine: liquid stone cast in place to your order for only three or four cents a pound! What a bargain!

Appropriateness

Anyone with an eye for the nature of things can recognize a quality of rightness—of appropriateness—when it appears in the use of a material. Specialists and amateurs alike know it when they are exposed to something that fits, and many of them are repelled when confronted with awkwardness or unnaturalness in a building. We all seem to have been born with the potential to know without being told when a thing is really right. Artists have an extra measure of this gift, and some develop it to an incredible degree. It is called by such sense-names as an *eye for painting*, an *ear for music*, a *feeling for architecture*, and *taste in clothes*. It does perhaps more than we suspect in keeping us from stepping too far out of line. This artificial world does little to help us develop our sense of rightness in things, but the sense is there if we listen carefully for it. Concrete construction can be brutally ugly; it can also be quite beautiful. The difference lies in its designer's sense of appropriateness and feelings about the material.

Paving

Sometimes, however, that sense is hard to find. We see new highways sweeping across the wild countryside and are moved at first by their beauty. The land seems somehow greener and more vast with a ribbon of white laid across it. When we are moved by such scenes a little warning light should go on, reminding us to consider their consequences—and then decide if the real costs are worth it.

It is obvious that conventional concrete or asphalt paving kills the land on which it lies. What isn't so obvious is the fact that it kills other land as well, not only by the polluting effects of its manufacture and of the street poisons it sends rushing away with the rainwater but also by the erosion its inevitable fast runoff causes. During a 1-inch rainstorm a single acre of paving can repel 26,000 gallons of fresh water, water intended to be held and used by the deep humus layers of natural ground covers, and then released, slowly, to nearby watercourses. No wonder our streams are in trouble.

Porous paving is a response, a good one, to overpaving. Its only fault is its high initial cost. That cost is somewhat offset by the savings in storm sewer costs made possible by the porous surfacing, but the savings don't begin to pay the premium. Porous pavements will have no measurable impact upon the country's water waste until their cost is more competitive with conventional, impervious paving and they become widely used. Attempts have been made to develop a porous *asphalt* paving but the results have not yet been very successful. Among the most widely used porous materials today are various types of open concrete blocks and open, waffle-pattern slabs of concrete, poured in place over single-use forms.

Crushed stone, of course, is the most common of all types of porous paving. It's also the cheapest, but it's dusty and noisy, it requires constant regrading, it can make driving dangerous at even moderate speeds, and it can't be cleared of snow very easily.

Porous, open paver-blocks, on the other hand, are relatively maintenance-free, clean, stable, strong, and easy to snowplow; and they allow grass to grow in their openings, offering greenness as well as good percolation. Their only physical problem is their tendency to get slightly misaligned by ice, temperature changes, and wheel loads, making moderate or high speed travel on them both uncomfortable and risky.

I've used a lot of porous paving blocks. They do a marvelous job, and they express the idea of land care far better than any impervious paving does. Information on porous paving materials can be found in some libraries, and in the office of almost every architect or landscape architect. The trouble is that most people don't feel they can simply walk into an architect's office and ask for such information. I often do it when I'm out of town and need a name or an address. I guess I've never stopped at a very big architectural office, but in every small or medium-size one I've visited, the people were more than happy to help me with such questions, and I seldom bothered to tell them I was an architect.

Petroleum-Based Products

The concrete I use on so many buildings is a product of tremendous heat, and many of the waterproofings and insulations I recommend are literally made out of oil. Each year it gets harder for me to justify my use of such things, but until we learn to grow buildings the way we do vegetables and trees, we will be forced to use considerable amounts of energy and great quantities of natural resources. There just isn't any practical way of escape from the manufactured world, and perhaps there shouldn't be. It's all a question of degree, of temperance, moderation, land respect, and self-restraint. The only way I know to make better decisions is to consider the probable world impact of each building during its projected lifetime.

Taking an extreme example, if you felled trees by hand and hewed the logs to build a cabin on the site, but then used electric heat to warm the leaky place each winter, you'd go deeper and deeper into environmental debt. If, on the other hand, you built a house of high-fuel-process concrete, and wrapped it with layers of petro-chemical-based waterproofing and insulation, but then used nothing but sunlight to heat the structure, the fuel saving might within a year or two equal all the fuels and resources that went into the mining, transporting, manufacturing, fabricating, and erection of the house. After that, you'd be home free in terms of energy, each year adding another bonus to the saving, as long as the house was used. The only trouble is that few comparisons are that obvious. It's far more likely to be a case of comparing gray areas to find the less harmful, less wasteful way.

Wood

One material we can probably use in good conscience at all times is actually manufactured by solar energy. The material *is*, in fact, stored sunlight, ready for use as either fuel or structure. I'm not certain as to the morality of using wood, but at the moment I have few qualms about it. These are some random thoughts on that bewitching material.

My most popular building designs, with few exceptions, have been wood framed. The rougher and more massive the timbers the more appealing the designs.

Wood surfaces often improve in appearance with age.

Wood is the only structural material that is also a good insulator.

FIG. 7.5 *Detail, McGeorge House, Moorestown, N.J., 1963*. (Artog)

FIG. 7.6 *View from mezzanine, Cherry Hill Library, 1965. Twelve-inch-square fir columns at 20-ft centers, 12- by 16-in beams, 3-in yellow pine decking, all rough-sawn. (Artog)*

Structures of heavy timber, while inflammable, will stand through fires that make limp spaghetti of structural steel.

Unlike concrete and steel frames, wood structures complain audibly about mistreatment; dangerous overloading brings forth creaks and groans long before failure occurs.

A half inch of glistening ice coats everything out-of-doors. The damage to trees seems extensive. Among the undamaged ones it seems impossible that branches can bend that far and live, but with the thaw, the branches recover.

Wood is our great renewable resource, they say, as they remove the trees and leave tortured soil to bake dry in the sun, to erode with the rains.

Wood is expensive.

The sale of wood stoves, particularly in places like New England where fuel oil prices are highest, is booming. And reforestation is occurring all over New England as more and more farms are abandoned.[1] Some ecologists fear the wood stove craze, and foresee the denuding of America's forests as a result. Here on Cape Cod I see more and more tracts from which all hardwoods have been removed for firewood. Still, there's a lot of forest land left. In Thoreau's time the Cape was bare, all of its original growth having been destroyed. It was still mostly bare in 1900, but now the Cape is a forested peninsula once more.

I hear conflicting news of the logging industry: Western Oregon is being devastated; Oregon is being reforested. I hear of vast timber stands in Alaska sold to foreign investors. But I also hear that Alaska's wilderness is mostly under federal protection.

Manhattan is a virgin forest; trees 200 feet tall are common there. Sparkling streams run through silent groves and pour into the Hudson. Wildlife abounds. That, at least, has been the *average* condition of the island for the last 10,000 years. Lately, however, something else seems to have happened there.

According to my postage records I mailed 1750 letters three years ago, 5300 the year before last, and 8900 last year. There is a communications explosion. Paper is one of its media. Paper is made from wood.

Today's project is the design of an environmental center for a university. The campus is 900 miles from my drawing board. Certain trees on the site will have to be removed (we don't say "killed" about trees) to make way for my environmental improvements, but there's often a lag of a year or two between the time of first design sketches and the start of construction. Do the condemned trees feel anything? Did they shiver, just now, when I drew that new contour line through the words "group of 20-inch cottonwoods" on the university site plan? And what about the west-coast trees destined to become the structural frame of the building? How carefully will they be removed? I changed the condition of an Oregon forest, this morning, by drawing some lines in Massachusetts. How many other architects are designing timber structures today?

A sawn two by four timber is insignificant only to people who do not know what the world was like before the advent of the power-driven saw; and a building of two products —brick and sawn lumber —is a social achievement whose true significance can only be grasped by people who have endured a smoke-filled dugout through a Massachusetts winter.

JAMES MARSTON FITCH

[1] *The New York Times,* Dec. 31, 1978.

CHAPTER EIGHT

Construction Practices

". . . and get rid of that!"

FIG. 8.1 *Used by permission, Richard Marek Publishers, © 1978.*

The Cary Arboretum

About 15 miles east of Poughkeepsie, New York, in the village of Mill-brook, there's a two-story building nestled so deeply into the sheltering earth that little more than its solar roof can be seen as you approach it. It's the Plant Science Building of the Cary Arboretum of the New York

Botanical Garden, a solar-heated office and lab building completed in 1979. The 1800-acre tract on which it stands and much of the money needed to establish the Arboretum were gifts of the Mary Flagler Cary Memorial Trust.

This project was the first of my designs to include all of the following:

Earth shelter
Solar heating
Thermal mass
Exterior insulation
Small north windows
Natural landscaping
Indoor operating shutters
Full exterior shading
Skylighting
Task lighting

FIG. 8.2 General view from the southwest, Plant Science Building, the Cary Arboretum of the New York Botanical Garden, 1978. (Artog)

FIG. 8.3 (above) *Courtyard framing, Cary Arboretum Plant Science Building (Artog)*

FIG. 8.4 (left) *Preliminary cross section, Plant Science Building, before skylights were added to provide all interior lighting.*

FIG. 8.5 *Interior, Plant Science Building. Ropes control pivoting insulating shutters at skylights.* (Artog)

It was also the first job of mine on which an attempt was made to go well beyond normal construction practices in the areas of site protection and waste management.* Among other things, the contractor was required to prepare and use large waste receptacles marked "Glass," "Plastic," "Steel," "Aluminum," and "Organic Wastes," to protect all stockpiled soils, to prevent erosion, to protect trees, to stay within carefully fenced work areas, and to prevent contamination of the soil by toxic materials.

*Fred Dubin's firm was responsible for the structural, mechanical, and electrical design. With the help of a gifted young architect named David Deppen I was able to do most of the rest. Interiors were done by Jim Dugan of Interspace, site planning by Environmental Planning and Design.

The results: only so-so. It was impossible to change the habits of American construction workers that quickly. They turned out to be just like the rest of us: spoiled, set in their ways, self-centered, and mostly unconcerned about the world. The environmental restrictions were, in many cases, disregarded. But a start was made. The little site damage which did occur was quickly corrected, and the construction workers were given another good reason to laugh at the silly and pompous breed called Architect. I had gone about it all so heavy-handedly it's a wonder I wasn't carried to the organic-wastes drum and discarded there myself. Without thinking it through, I had assumed that my environmental priorities, which took years—decades—to develop, would be accepted instantly by hundreds of strangers simply because I'd added a new section to the construction specifications. Obviously needed are more and better ways to sell site husbandry to the workers, and interesting—even funny—ways to make it routine practice. For example, the job might have started with a film, documenting the devastation caused at other construction projects, followed by a conference of all the building trades people—mechanics *and* laborers as well as the supervisors. The campaign would have been kept alive, as the work proceeded, through the use of cartoon posters appealing for site protection; there would also be better waste-drum labeling, tighter dollar controls on the general contractor, and even regular land-husbandry bonuses. If the whole campaign were sponsored by the building trades unions themselves, so much the better, for what promotes more and better future work than successful work today?

Indoor Shutters

My first indoor surprise on that project was the amount of condensation that formed on the inner surfaces of windows and skylights in the wintertime when the indoor insulating shutters were closed. I suspect that the water and ice that formed on each pane came primarily from room moisture leaking through and around the shutter and condensing on the glass, rather than from the water vapor contained in the small body of room air trapped in the shuttered space. On winter mornings, when the shutters were first opened, paper-thin sheets of ice and drops of 33-degree water slid and dripped from the skylights and the windows. The problem has already tended to correct itself somewhat; much of the condensation was probably the excess moisture that only brand-new buildings, particularly brand-new concrete buildings, contain. It does illustrate, however, the way "solutions" often tend to generate new troubles. Fortunately, this condensation was far, far less of a problem than the heat-loss that would otherwise have occurred. It shows, too, that we may never find a complete solution to any problem. As long as we stumble in the general direction of improvement, perhaps that's all we can ask.

Several corrections are already under consideration with regard to that condensation matter. They'll be tested, and the better ones among them will then be used. One is to provide condensate pans or spongy pads at all sill levels to allow the water to evaporate back into the room air again before the moisture does any structural damage. Another is to provide little drains from windowsills and skylights, and a third is to seal the shutters even more tightly against vapor. (A fourth would be to do away with the insulating shutters, but, as I've said, the heat losses then would be unconscionable.)

Ah, if only every architect could have an arboretum staff with its huge greenhouse and nursery and its horticultural experts ready to adorn his work, inside and out, with masses of living plants! What a difference they've made! Instead of taking years to heal, the earth wounds were gone and the building made photogenic by the time the builders had left.

The Cow-Manure Cocktail

Then there was the infamous cow-manure cocktail. Apparently it's a secret formula used by landscape experts to give new stone walls the weathered look of great age in just a few weeks. When I aired a mild displeasure with the uniformly new and cold-looking cement finish on the building's exterior, someone gave me the recipe: mix a few pounds of fresh cow manure with water in a 55-gallon drum, let the mixture age in the sun for a couple of weeks, and then splash it onto the wall. When I arranged to have a sample batch made and tested—before allowing the entire building to be given a barn smell—I found to my disappointment that the cement plaster was too smooth, or that it dried out too quickly, or that it was in some other way unresponsive to such improvement, and the cocktail method was abandoned. I decided to do it the right way and let nature take its course, each year adding more blue washes below the copper sheets, more rust tones whenever bits of iron were overlooked, more grays from the American sky, and more greens as mosses from the rain slowly do their work.

To tell you the truth, I'm still not even certain that I wasn't being had by the man who recommended the cow-manure treatment. It sounds in retrospect a little too much like the advice I once got from my grandmother when, on her farm as a teenager, I expressed impatience with the slow growth of my first whiskers, particularly the ones of my future moustache: "Rub a little chicken dirt on your upper lip and you'll have a moustache in no time." I don't care to say whether or not I followed her advice.

Wood Preservatives

At the Arboretum all the giant timbers were to have been specially treated against rotting. In fact, I have certificates from the wood-treatment company to the effect that they were—thoroughly and in the specified way. But I've learned not to put utter faith in the wood preservation process. The very best material was specified, the stuff for impregnating wood when it is to be placed in direct contact with the earth, not high above a courtyard as much of this wood now is. LP-22 is what the American Wood Preservers Institute calls the process, and it certainly did sound good when I read about it. But when the timbers arrived it was quickly apparent that some had received only partial coverage. When they were cut we could see that the treatment had penetrated only a small fraction of an inch, and when we checked on the required recoating of all newly sawed or drilled surfaces, we found that many had been overlooked by the people responsible for the job. *Proper* wood treatment does, of course, protect wood. Think of all the piers, the telephone poles, and the seawalls that last for years under fierce conditions. Think of all the wood foundations used so widely in the Midwest.

But what are the environmental penalties of such resource-conserving practices? What are the treatment materials made of? Where does the manufacturer dump his wastes? Do treated members poison the earth around them, and, if they do, how long does this poisoning last? Does it get into water supplies? Is it hazardous to the people working on or near the treated members? I hate to think what the answers to these questions might be, just as I hate to think how much termite poison is used in the United States each year. No one seems to have any idea what we are doing to ourselves. I still use these poisons and preservatives occasionally when no alternative is available, hoping that someone more responsible than I is in full control of the American poison situation.

It is always better to use wood in such a way that it is *naturally* protected from rot and insects. Metal termite shields, good ventilation around the material, dry joints, and separation of all wood from contact with the earth should always be the chosen practice, poison being held in reserve until proven necessary. It's not always possible, but all too often we overkill before exploring the gentler alternatives.

Special Insulations

There are large, insulated, waterproofed concrete tanks buried in the

Plant Science Building's courtyard. Two are for the storage of hot, sometimes almost boiling, water from the rooftop solar collectors, and one is for the storage of rainwater for fire protection and site irrigation use. The tanks offered an almost insoluble design challenge because there is to my knowledge no foolproof technique for dealing with that type of installation. Imagine the expansion and contraction and all the stresses involved when, on a winter day with an outdoor temperature of zero, the water in the tank only a few inches away from the open air may be more than 200° warmer! We checked with high-temperature insulation contractors, special waterproofings manufacturers, refineries, and solar designers. When we'd find a solution to one part of the problem it would usually turn out to be incompatible with the solution to another part. The result is a hodgepodge of different insulations having networks of vent slots, joints using all kinds of flexible connections, coverings, and inspection manholes, and a weathering surface of reinforced cement plaster to cover it all. The combination seems to work, but if the theroretical temperature ranges that evolved midway through the construction period had been available at the outset, I'm sure that all the water now stored underground would be stored in well-insulated, standard metal tanks *inside* a conventional basement from which inspections and repairs could be made more easily.

Thank God for the clients we had! They realized from the start that theirs would in many ways be an experimental building and they were willing to help advance the state of this dinosaur art called architecture, not only by using, but also by monitoring, the performance of our innovations.

The Act of Construction

Almost none of the architectural schools teach anything about the ravages of the construction act itself. Very few architects, or architects' specifications, mention the things that should be done to protect a site when the builders are there. Take, for instance, the green space outside the work area. Can anything other than fencing be used to protect it? Proper fencing can control the movements of two-legged creatures and wheeled vehicles, but it will do nothing to stop fire or runoff. In the first case, firelanes should be cut around construction perimeters so that fires caused by construction activities will not tend to spread into the terribly vulnerable green areas around them. Erosion, siltation, and the polluting effects of contruction-chemical runoff can be controlled by the use of low dikes or mounds surrounding the construction site, and of course deep mulching does a marvelous job of preventing erosion.

Wildlife

With regard to wildlife, the main thing is to be sure that, if poisons are used to control rats and mice within a building site, the poisons not be placed where they are accessible to other animals. That's a tough one, but it can be done. Competent advice from such sources as local museums of natural history should be sought on the subject before blind attempts are made to do things with such long-lasting consequences.

Poisons

Chemicals, oils, solvents: These are the kinds of things common to construction sites that can cause terrible damage to the soil or to watercourses. If there's a concrete-mixing plant on the site the potential for environmental damage is even greater; its runoff can be extremely harmful. The areas in which such destructive materials are stored and used must be carefully diked so they can't leach their poisons into the living world. Then, at the completion of contruction, they must be carefully cleaned up and the refuse buried or removed. Removal, of course, presumes safe disposal elsewhere. If that is not likely, on-site neutralization, detoxification, and burial are probably the best ways to dispose of these substances.

Topsoil

I was surprised to discover, several years back, that topsoil is actually a living creature, full of bacteria, enzymes, decaying plant materials, insects and spores. Topsoil lives for centuries—for eons—and is the source of each site's great life-supporting potential. We wouldn't kill an elephant if we found it on a construction site, and topsoil has more value in most respects. Don't allow it to become mixed with subsoil or other materials. Pile it carefully, clear of all pollutants. Dike the foot of the pile to prevent erosion and creepage, and either seed its slopes with annual grasses, if a growth season is likely to occur during the life of the stockpile, or cover it with mulch.

Water Management

Very often, during the course of a construction project, there just isn't enough mulch available to cover all the exposed areas. In such cases it's necessary to create flat grades—especially on hillsides—to create diked, flat terraces so that the rainwater will not rush away but will be held by the soil until it can either evaporate or percolate. Temporary water-conservation pits are also helpful. They can be built to hold great quantities of muddy, construction runoff water until it can settle out its solids and be drained away slowly as clear water. If subsoil is covered with mulch, even wastepaper mulch, the soil's tendency to erode by wind or water will be greatly reduced.

Tree Removal

Plan tree removal carefully. First, the trees are felled, leaving a foot or two of stump projecting from the ground. The felled trees are then stripped of their branches. The branches are piled in one place, and the trunks are cut into 6-ft lengths and stacked in another. Then the stumps are pulled. The branches and leaves (and of course any natural forest litter that was on the site) should be chipped or pulped by a machine capable of reducing it all to some kind of mulch. The trunks can be cut into firewood or into planks, and the stumps—well, the stumps seem to have no immediate usefulness, which is perhaps a benefit to the land. If there is space on the site, the stumps should be piled there, not buried under loads of fill, but piled in the open, where they can slowly rot back into the soil, forming for many years an ideal wildlife cover and landscape backdrop.

The number-one rule, however, is to save every possible tree, because the miracles it performs are almost uncountable, and trees are not very quickly replaced. Fencing is the only dependable way to protect trees slated to be saved. No mere marker can prevent the encroachments that spell death to a tree. Scarring or bumping of the trunk, driving over the roots, changing grades too close to the tree—any of these can kill it. Because of the sizes and kinds of machines used in the construction of modern buildings it's almost impossible to count on saving any trees within 15 or even 20 feet of a new building's walls. Better to concentrate on the trees more than 15 feet from the walls, making sure that no silty runoff, or construction traffic, or contaminant can damage these precious creatures.

Respect for Resources

The main reason for segregating wastes at a construction site is neither organic nor cosmetic: it's educational. If everyone involved in a project can be reminded, constantly, of the importance of the materials he touches, then that respect will begin to be expressed in the building he builds, and in his own life. If his kids must do the same things each day at school, and if you and I and everyone else must do it, we may all begin to take second looks at what we so casually discard. We can't reshape the nation's waste management practices by segregating a few wastes at construction sites. The problem is so vast we may need a revolution to solve it. But the revolution will never start if everyone waits for someone else. Construction industry waste is notorious. We're involved in construction. This is where *we've* got to start.

Placing Earth on Roofs

Very few underground buildings are built by the use of mining techniques—that is, by tunneling into the sides of hills or digging deep into the earth. Almost every underground building in America is constructed by a method we call "cut and cover": we dig a hole, build the building and then bury it in earth. Obviously a great deal of care has to go into the final covering of waterproofed and insulated rooftops. The materials in these two layers are extremely fragile, and the good performance of each is essential to the success of the building. If either the waterproofing or the insulation is damaged, its effectiveness is likely to be lost, and the work must be redone. That's why earthen fill must be placed just so, covering the insulation boards in such a way that they are not dislodged, broken, or crushed, and without letting bits of earth get between and under them to disturb their alignment and invite roots and rodents to damage the building envelope. Assuming that you want to use, as fill material, earth that was stockpiled for that purpose, the question is how to get it from the stockpile to the roof. Bulldozers can't do it: they're far too heavy. There seems as yet to be no simple way to carry out this procedure.

On small jobs, it's possible to use a conveyer belt to move earth onto a roof, where, by hand labor, it can then be spread to the desired grade. It's the kind of work one wouldn't want to do every day; double handling—by hand—is both expensive and inefficient.

Another way to place earth on a roof is by the use of a crane—the *careful* use of a crane, that is. Because of its great weight, the earth must be placed—not dropped—in small piles, well-distributed over the entire roof, from which it can then, with relatively little additional effort, be pushed down to the desired level, and spread by hand.

To design a roof strong enough to carry the moving, vibrating weight of a bulldozer would involve an intolerable waste of building materials, for, after that once-in-a-century ordeal, most of the structure's load-carrying capacity would never be needed again. One way to provide for the weight of an earth-moving machine on the roof of a building, without adding enormously to the roof's structure and cost, is to place temporary shoring under those portions of the roof on which the machinery will work, but the entire process must be extremely well thought-out and coordinated, for a single mistake could spell disaster. Shoring is relatively inexpensive, and, compared to other techniques, its use in some cases may save money. But the design of the shoring must not be based on guesswork. Tremendously complex forces are involved when great weights are in motion, and the calculations required must be performed by a competent structural engineer.

Some "underground" roofs are now being covered by deep mulch alone, up to two feet of it, in order to have the benefits (insulation, water retention, wild flowers) without the drawback (weight) of earth cover. So far, these experiments look promising, but the mulch will need replacement from time to time as it compresses and decays.

Similarly, the use of lightweight materials such as vermiculite to reduce the weight of rooftop soils is also gaining favor.* The material is not cheap, however, and the process of mixing it with on-site earth fill to reduce the cost can be tedious.

Another technique with high potential is that of doing everything, from the building of the roof structure to its final landscaping, right at ground level, and then jacking the entire assembly, hydraulically, to its proper position. This technique allows much fuller use of heavy machinery in many stages of the contruction and may, in certain areas and on certain jobs, be cheaper and better than building in the conventional way. There was quite a rash of this lift-slab construction—without earth cover, of course—about a generation ago, but it came to little. Maybe now, with this added reason for lifting the completed slab, the economy and great strength of hydraulics will bring the process into more common use.

Keeping Earth on Roofs

Closely related to the matter of placing earth on the roof is keeping it there—erosion prevention, in other words. If the raw earth on the roof is not sloped back at the edges to its own inherent "angle of repose," and if that slope is not immediately protected, it can be severly eroded by the first rainstorm. The best provision for this is to cover all such earth surfaces, as soon as they reach their final grades, with deep layers of mulch. The mulch may be of any kind—any organic matter that's been finely chopped, pulped, shredded, rotted, or arranged so as to hold moisture rather than let it rush away, carrying with it great quantities of the

*Roger D. Moore, a professor of landscape architecture at the University of Georgia (Athens, GA 30602), is one of those doing important work in this field.

carefully placed earth. In my experience the best mulching material of all is of the pine needle kind, particularly when it has partially decomposed. It will hold its place on many sloping surfaces, even newly placed ones, during heavy cloudbursts. But mulch of any sort—compost, humus, peat moss, spoiled hay, even chopped paper waste—can be used to launch the restoration of land. Mulching often gives dead land all the chance it needs to revive the ancient processes we now associate with organic health. Adding manure to the mulch offers an even better chance.

I have seen far too many jobs on which contractors tried to protect newly placed rooftop earth by the use of plastic sheets or a few bales of hay, only to find that rain is not that easily thwarted. Water always wins when we try to impose human laws on natural systems. Sooner or later all of our contrived schemes must fail if they contradict the ground rules of the natural world.

If only we could look a century ahead for a moment! It would show us, instantly, the solutions to architectural and construction problems we're now bound to grope for with an embarrassingly high failure rate. A hundred years from now, this book will seem impossibly naive, its readers unable to believe that we could have been so blind only a few generations earlier. Whether or not *our* shortcomings will remind those readers of their own is anyone's guess. All we can be sure of is that neither we nor they nor their own descendants will ever arrive at a perfect architecture.

We participate in a process which simply continues—upward, we hope—not only in architecture but in all other worthy human pursuits.

CHAPTER NINE

The Last Page

We feel obliged to fill time. If there is nothing at hand to fill it with, then we manufacture filler. (Look how we spend our days.) Meanwhile, the most beautiful world we'll ever know slides deeper into trouble. Four billion of us, simply by living here, are greasing its skids—four *billion* of us, all serving ourselves first. Statistically, there seems to be no hope at all. No government, no religion, certainly no new architecture, is going to set things right. Even a sudden switch to the most enlightened, the gentlest, of architectures would make only a small dent in the overall problem. Nuclear catastrophe, nuclear radiation, toxins, waste, land abuse—none of them would be changed.

"We shape our buildings, and our buildings shape us," said Churchill. I disagree. Many of us are unmoved by even the most dramatic of structures; architecture, being but an expression of human values, cannot be expected to turn us around and lead us to higher levels. The values have to come first.

If it were left up to us—architects, builders, the entire construction industry—to set things right, there would be no hope at all. And yet there *is* hope. As the awareness of consequences spreads among us it is being expressed not just in how we build but in how we work and travel and play, in what we eat and wear, and in the way we feel about our shared future here. Those expressions will be something to see, all right, and they may just manage to nudge us up over the edge, onto the next level, wherever and whatever that is to be.

Our principal impediments at present are neither lack of energy or material resources nor of essential physical and biological knowledge. Our principal constraints are cultural.

DONALD WATSON

A Brief Architectural Tour
of the United States

1. Fresno, CA: The Underground Gardens of Baldassare Forestiere.
2. Sea Ranch, CA: Works by David Wright.
3. Scottsdale, AZ: Paolo Soleri's "Cosanti."
4. Scottsdale, AZ: Frank Lloyd Wright's "Taliesin West."
5. Cordes Junction, AZ: Paolo Soleri's "Arcosanti."
6. Choco Canyon, NM: Ancient Indian solar site.
7. Interior, SD: The Badlands.
8. Minneapolis, MN: Butler Square, restored brick and timber ware-houses.
9. Minneapolis, MN: The Underground Space Center of the University of Minnesota.
10. Spring Green, WI: Frank Lloyd Wright's "Taliesin."
11. Madison, WI: Many works by Frank Lloyd Wright.
12. Racine, WI: Corporate Headquarters, S. C. Johnson & Son, Inc.
13. Milwaukee, WI: Wildflower gardens of Lorrie Otto, 9701 N. Lake Drive.
14. Chicago, IL: Many works by Frank Lloyd Wright.
15. Detroit, MI: Renaissance Center (beautiful concrete designs suggest possibilities for underground spaces).
16. Ohiopyle, PA: Frank Lloyd Wright's "Fallingwater."
17. New York, NY: Frank Lloyd Wright's Guggenheim Museum.
18. New York, NY: Eero Saarinen's TWA terminal.
19. Millbrook, NY: Wells's Plant Science Building, Carey Arboretum.
20. Hatchville, MA: The New Alchemy Institute.
21. FL: The underground houses of William Morgan.

NOTE: Many of these places have brief and sometimes unusual visiting hours. It is advisable to make complete arrangements in advance. Addresses and telephone numbers are available at AIA offices and local chambers of commerce.

A Malcolm Wells Chronology

Date	Publication Data	Author	Title/Subject
January 1959	*AIA Journal,* vol. 31, no. 1, pp. 38-39	Malcolm Wells	"Don't Forget the Toilet Rooms!" (architectural registration exams)
April 1962	*Progressive Architecture,* vol. 62, no. 4, pp. 178-181	—	"Masonry Interiors" (Wells House, Cherry Hill, N.J.)
October 1962	*House Beautiful,* pp. 83-93	Curtis Besinger	"Cover Story: It Looks Traditional But Is It?" (Wells House, Cherry Hill, N.J.)
Spring-Summer 1963	*House Beautiful Building Manual,* vol. 45, pp. 104-114	—	"Cover Story: It Looks Traditional But Is It?" (Wells House, Cherry Hill, N.J.)
April 1964	*Progressive Architecture,* vol. 44, no. 4, pp. 163-166	—	"Fully Air-Conditioned Plant In Florida" (RCA Factory, Palm Beach Gardens)
October 1964	*House Beautiful,* pp. 83, 101	James DeLong	"Architectural Forecast" (Wells House, Cherry Hill, N.J.)
February 1965	*Progressive Architecture,* vol. 45, no. 2, pp. 174-179	Malcolm Wells	"Nowhere To Go But Down" (underground architecture)
Autumn 1966	*Horizon,* vol. 8, no. 4, pp. 64	Wendy Buehr	"New Designs for Megalopolis" (underground architecture)
January-February 1968	*Charette,* vol. 48, no. 1	Malcolm Wells	"Penn's Sylvania" (underground architecture)
February 1968	*Philadelphia Magazine,* vol. 59, no. 2, pp. 61-66	—	"Ever Upward" (state mottoes)
March 1968	*Philadelphia Magazine,* vol. 59, no. 3, pp. 146-156	Barry Rosenberg	"The Underground Man" (Malcolm Wells)
March 1968	*Progressive Architecture,* vol. 49, no. 3, pp. 164-165	Malcolm Wells	"Down Under, Down Under . . . or: How Not to Build Underground" (Australian opal miners' houses)
May 1968	*Crosswinds,* vol. 1, no. 1, pp. 12-13	Joe Gagen	"The Underground Church" (a Wells proposal)
September 15, 1968	*Discover,* the Philadelphia Sunday Bulletin magazine, pp. 6-9	Malcolm Wells	"Off We Go Into the (cough) Wild Blue Yonder" (waste management)
June 26, 1969	*Iron Age,* p. 61	Scott Hockenberry	"Can Industry and Nature Coexist?" (Wells's proposals)
June 1969	World Wildlife Fund, 16 pp.	Malcolm Wells	"What You Can Do, Right Now, About The Mess We Live In"

Date	Publication Data	Author	Title/Subject
August 1969	*Building Progress,* pp. 12-13	—	"Architect's Hideaway" (Wells Cherry Hill, N.J., office)
September 1969	*Architectural and Engineering News,* p. 70	—	"Names" (Malcolm Wells)
September 8, 1969	*Age* (Melbourne, Austrailia, newspaper), p. 10	Graham Whitford	"They're Going Down, Now" (Wells's work)
November 1969	*Philadelphia Magazine,* vol. 60, no. 11, pp. 106-110	Malcolm Wells	"The Semantics of Pollution: Too Much Crap."
January 1970	*Philadelphia Magazine,* vol. 61, no. 1, pp. 94-97	Rosalie Wright	"For The 70's I Predict" (Wells and others look ahead)
September 1970	*Philadelphia Magazine,* vol. 61, no. 9, pp. 45-48	Malcolm Wells (pen name Roy Taylor)	"Getting Sterile" (vasectomy)
October 1970	*Waverly Gazette* Victoria, Australia), p. 13	Malcolm Wells	"Lawns, The Destroyers"
October 5, 1970	*A/S* (AIA student association), vol. 8, pp. 4-5	—	"Wilderness Is A Living Community"
October 28, 1970	*Waverly Gazette* (Victoria Australia), p. 26	—	"The Grass Is Greener, But" (problems caused by lawns)
November 1970	(Self) Malcolm Wells publication 11 pp.	—	"Ecological Standards for Construction"
December 8, 1970	*A/S* (AIA student association), vol. 9, pp. 9-10	—	"Architecture Based on Wilderness Values"
January 1971	*Museum News,* vol. 49, no. 5, pp. 9-11	—	"Eschatology: The Last Word Exhibit Themes" (ecoarchitectu for museums)
February 1971	*Architecture In Australia,* p. 76	—	"The Challenge of Wilderness"
1971	(Self) Malcolm Wells publication 32 pp.	—	"The Great Ecological Coloring Book of Death and Life and Architecture"
1971	(Self)	—	"Hockey Sticks Mean Trouble" (frightening curves on graphs)
March 1971	*Progressive Architecture,* vol. 52, no. 3, pp. 92-97	—	"The Absolutely Constant Incontestably Stable Architectu Value Scale" (wilderness value
May-June 1971	*Architect* (Australian RAIA Magazine) vol. 3, no. 4, pp. 20-21	—	"The Great Ecological Coloring Book of Death and Life and Architecture" (condensation)
June 2, 1971	*Waverly Gazette* (Victoria, Australia) p. 14	—	"The Birds of Bellazonne" (wa management)

Date	Publication Data	Author	Title/Subject
September 1971	*Building Ideas* (Australia) pp. 2-7	—	"Malcolm Wells—Building Without Destroying The Land"
December 1971	*Progressive Architecture,* vol. 52, no. 12, pp. 80-81	—	"The Facts of Life". (review of Ian McHarg book)
January 8 1972	*Environmental Action Bulletin* (Rodale) pp. 4-5	—	"An Environmentally Sound Architecture Is Possible"
January 1972	*Doors and Hardware* vol. 36, no. 5, pp. 8-9	—	"Cavity Catch" (an invention by Wells)
July 1972	*Architectural Design* (Britain) pp. 433-434	—	"An Ecologically Sound Architecture Is Possible"
July 1972	*Building Official and Code Administrator* pp. 4-8	—	"The Architects are Killing Us!"
August 1972	*Environmental Quality Magazine* pp. 29-32	—	"Undertaking With a Green Thumb" (ecological burial)
March 1973	*Harper's Magazine* vol. 246, no. 1474, pp. 86-97	—	"We'll Have The Five-day Forecast After This Brief Message" (weather forecast perversions)
Summer 1973	*A/S* (AIA Student Association) vols. 18, 19, p. 11	—	"Light and Shiny vs. Thick and Heavy" (underground architecture)
July 1973	*Environmental Quality Magazine* pp. 51-57	—	"Confessions of a Gentle Architect" (underground office)
November 1973	*Christian Living,* vol. 20, no. 11, pp. 2-5	Jean M. Wyness	"Malcolm Wells' Blueprint for A Greener World"
1974, 1975, 1976	*Discover,* The Philadelphia Sunday Bulletin Magazine	Wells	(regular twice-a-month column on environmental subjects.)
February 3, 1974	*Discover* (see above) pp. 6-7, 12-13	Tilly Spetgang	"No One Loves Sun and Rain and Green Life more than Mac Wells So He Builds Underground"
June 1974	*Progressive Architecture,* vol. 55, no. 6, pp. 59-63, 112-113	Wells	"Environmental Impact" (runoff, underground architecture, Wells's office)
September 1974	*Mainliner* (United Air Lines Magazine) vol. 18, no. 9, pp. 28-31	—	"What Your Home Will Be Like In Fifty Years"
April 1975	Edmund Scientific Company Barrington, N.J.	Homan, Thomason, Wells	*Solaria.* $24.95. Item no 9469 (description and plans of solar/earth-covered house)
July 1975	Solar Service Corporation Cherry Hill, N.J.	Tilly Spetgang	*Tilly's Catch-A-Sunbeam Coloring Book* $1.50 (illustrated by Wells)

Date	Publication Data	Author	Title/Subject
September 1975	*A & U* (Japanese architecture magazine)	—	(special article on low-energy architecture including work by Wells.)
October 1975	*Werk* (Swiss architecture magazine) pp. 103-141	Pierre Zoelly	"L'Architecture Souterraine" (including work by Wells)
December-January 1975-1976	*National Mall Monitor* vol. 5, no. 6, pp. 4, 25	—	(underground shopping center proposals by Wells)
November 1975	*Runners' World* vol. 10, no. 11, pp. 23-24	Wells	"Foot Power and Its Future"
November 1975	*Science Digest* pp. 31-42	Richard Dempewolff	(underground architecture, including work by Wells)
February 22, 1976	*The New York Times* p. D1	Wendy Schulman	"Malcolm Wells and His underground Office"
February 1976	*The Futurist,* vol. 10, no. 1, pp. 20-24	Wells	"Why I Went Underground"
March 1976	Edmund Scientific Company	Irwin Spetgang and Malcolm Wells	*Your Home's Solar Potential* $9.95
April 1976	*Solar Age,* vol. 1, no. 4, pp. 15-17	Nancy Homan	"Solaria"
May 1976	Edmund Scientific Company	Wells	*Energy Essays* $5.95
Spring-Summer 1976	*House Beautiful Building Manual*	—	"Being An Architect May Not Seem Like Much of A Sin"
August 1976	*Japan Architecture*	—	(underground architecture, including work by Wells
May-June 1976	*Your Church,* pp. 21-22, 59-61	Richard L. Critz	"Interview: Malcolm Wells"
July 1976	National Science Foundation	Frank Moreland	The Use of Earth-Covered Buildings $3.25 (U.S. Government Printing Office NS RA 760006 including work by Wells)
July 1976	Cary Arboretum	Robert Goodland	*Buildings and the Environment* (including work by Wells)
Fall 1976	*The CoEvolution Quarterly,* pp. 26-36	Wells	"Underground Architecture"
September 1976	*Solar Age*	Van Der Meer	"Down to Earth Housing" (including work by Wells)
March 1977	*Popular Mechanics* pp. 80-81, 140-146	Richard Dempewolff	(underground houses, including work by Wells)
April 1977	*Popular Science* pp. 88-89	Elaine Smay	(underground houses, including work by Wells)
April 1977	*Organic Gardening* p. 121	—	(review of work by Wells)

Date	Publication Data	Author	Title/Subject
May 1977-April 1980	(self-published)	Wells	Underground Designs, 8th printing $6.00 ppd. (Bx 1149, Brewster, MA 02631)
November 1977	*Popular Science* p. 131	Richard Stepler	(review of *Underground Designs*)
April 1978	Rodale Press	Irwin Spetgang and Malcolm Wells	*How to Buy Solar Heating Without Getting Burnt* $6.95
June 1978	The CoEvolution Quarterly	J. Baldwin	*Soft Tech* $5.00 (including reprint of Wells' 1976 "Underground Architecture)
August 1978	Rodale Press	James McCullagh	*Ways To Play* $6.95 (last chapter, "The Body," by Wells
November 1978	*AIA Journal* vol. 67, no. 13 pp. 35-37	Andrea Dean	"Malcolm Wells and His Solaria"
Winter 1978	*Verbatim,* vol. 5, no. 3, pp. 8-9	Wells	"The B-P List"
Winter 1979	*Popular Science* p. 23	Irwin Spetgang and Malcolm Wells	*Solar Energy Handbook* "Homeowners' Guide to Avoid Solar Ripoffs"
April 1979	*Solar Age,* pp. 6-10	Bill D'Alessandro	"Sky Mining at The Cary Arboretum"
April 1979	*Progressive Architecture* pp. 71-73	—	"The Cary Arboretum"
November-December 1979	Compost Science/Land Utilization pp. 40-41	Wells	"The Town Dump"
January 1980	*Consumers' Research,* pp. 11-12	—	"Going Underground" (including work by Wells)
Spring 1980	Van Nostrand Reinhold	—	*Notes From The Energy Underground*
Spring 1980	Taplinger Publishing	Kappy Wells, Connie Simo, Malcolm Wells	*Sandtiquity* (beach structures)
1974	WPVI-TV, Channel 6, Philadelphia	Jon Miller Producer	*Assignment: Malcolm Wells* 30 minutes. (Construction of Wells' Cherry Hill underground office) *Videotape.*
1976	Cary Arboretum, Millbrook, NY	Ann Eisner, Director. Vision Assoc.	*A Gift of Land.* 27 minutes. (Story of the founding of the arboretum, including commentary by Wells). *Film.*
1978	Cary Arboretum	Griffen Productions	A Building In The Sun. 20 minutes. (Construction of the Cary Plant Science Building) *Film.*

Marginal Quotation Credits

PAGE 29   Robert Venturi, *Complexity and Contradiction in Architecture,* New York Graphic Society, 1977.

PAGE 38   James Marston Fitch, *American Building 2: The Environmental Forces That Shape It,* Houghton Mifflin, Boston, 1975. Reprinted with permission.

PAGE 41   James Marston Fitch, *American Building 2: The Environmental Forces That Shape It,* Houghton Mifflin, Boston, 1975. Reprinted with permission.

PAGE 43   Suzanne Stephens, Introduction Part II, "Formal Dynamics," *Progressive Architecture,* vol. 60, no. 4, April 1979, p. 116.

PAGE 43   James Marston Fitch, *American Building 1: The Historical Forces That Shaped It,* 2d ed., Houghton Mifflin, Boston, 1966. Reprinted with permission.

PAGE 43   John Ruskin quoted in James Marston Fitch, *American Building 1: The Historical Forces That Shaped It,* 2d ed., Houghton Mifflin, Boston, 1966. Reprinted with permission.

PAGE 44   James Marston Fitch, *American Building 1: The Historical Forces That Shaped It,* 2d ed. Houghton Mifflin, Boston, 1966. Reprinted with permission.

PAGE 46   Ada Louise Huxtable, "Philip Johnson and the Temper of These Times," *The New York Times,* May 13, 1979, p. 27. Reprinted with permission.

PAGE 52   Richard Crowther, "Conclusion: The Future Is Rich," *Progressive Architecture,* vol. 60, no. 4, April 1979, p. 144.

PAGE 71   William Morgan, "Up to Earth," *Progressive Architecture,* vol. 60, no. 4, April 1979, p. 87.

PAGE 71   Donald Watson, "Three Perspectives on Energy," *Architectural Record,* vol. 65, no. 1, January 1979, p. 126.

PAGE 86   Vernon E. Jordan, Jr., *The New York Times,* May 5, 1979. Reprinted with permission.

PAGE 89   James Marston Fitch, *American Building 1: The Historical Forces That Shaped It.* 2d ed., Houghton Mifflin, Boston, 1966. Reprinted with permission.

PAGE 109   Donald Watson, "Three Perspectives on Energy," *Architectural Record,* vol. 165, no. 1, January 1979, p. 126.

PAGE 109   Philip Steadman, *Energy, Environment, and Building,* a report to the Academy of Natural Sciences, Philadelphia, Syndicate of the Cambridge University Press, Cambridge, England, p. 5.

PAGE 109   Donald Watson, "Three Perspectives on Energy," *Architectural Record,* vol. 165, no. 1, January 1979, p. 125.

PAGE 150   James Marston Fitch, *American Building 1: The Historical Forces That Shaped It,* 2d ed., Houghton Mifflin, Boston, 1966. Reprinted with permission.

PAGE 165   Donald Watson, "Three Perspectives on Energy," *Architectural Record,* vol. 165, no. 1, January 1979, p. 127.

Index

National Council of Architectural Registration Boards, 60
Natural landscapes, 99–100
Neighborliness, 53–54
New Alchemy Institute, 29, 64
New Inventions in Low-Cost Solar Heating (Shurcliff), 122
New Jersey:
   Cherry Hill underground office buildings, 17, 23, 25–27
   Collingswood Church of Christ, 23
   Mt. Laurel decision, 56
   Pine Barrens, 94–96
New York:
   Cary Aboretum, 133, 151–158
   wilderness in Manhattan, 37
   World's Fair (1964), 22, 85
New York AIA chapter, 5
New York Botanical Garden, 133, 151–158
Noise, 128–131
Nondegradation of land, 54, 94–97
North-sloping sites, 118–119
Nuclear power, 9, 48, 53, 93

Ohio, Locust Hill House, 132–133
Overpaving, 67–68

Paving, 89–92, 146–147
   overpaving, 67–68
   porous, 58, 146–147
   statistics of, 91, 146
Pennsylvania:
   Philadelphia, 68–69, 94
   Three Mile Island, 9, 93
Pennsylvania, University of, 32
Percolation beds, 13, 15, 102–105
Petroleum-based products, 147–148
Philadelphia (Pa.), 68–69, 94
Pine Barrens (N.J.), 94–96
Plants, green, 19
Plastics, 53
Poisons at construction site, 159
Pollution controls, 9, 30, 48, 53, 96
Prodigious Builders, The (Rudofsky), 49n., 63
Progressive Architecture, 16n., 109, 137
Psychological ramifications of gentle architecture, 58–59

R factors, of soil, 135
Radiation protection, 135

Rasmussen, S. E., 45n.
Rats, 117–118
Raven Rocks (Ohio), 132–133
Recertification of architects, 59–61
Resources:
   foreign, 135–136
   respect for, 160–161
Retention basins, 102–105
Rockefeller, Abby, 133–134
Roofs:
   collapse of, 98
   earth placed on, 29, 70, 161–163
Roots, 117–118
Rudofsky, Bernard, 49, 62–63
Runoffs, 68–70
Ruskin, John, 43

Safety as the architectural priority, 64–65
Sand structures, 51–52
Sandtiquity (Wells, Simo, Wells), 51
Sanitary land fill, 96
Sewerless toilets, 32
Sex factors in architecture, 10–12
Ships, liquified natural gas, 115
Shopping centers, 14, 30
Shurcliff, William A., 63, 122
Shutters, indoor and insulating, 155–156
Silver, Nathan, 46
Simo, Connie, 51
Site selection, 105–107
Slums, 19
Small structures, 31
Small windows, 119–120
Soft Tech, 63
Soil, 39, 112–113, 134–135
Solar greenhouses, 132–133
Solar-Heated Buildings of North America (Shurcliff), 63
Solar heating, 29, 32, 39, 122
Solar Home Book, The (Anderson), 63
Soleri, Paolo, 31
Spetgang, Irwin, 132
Steadman, Philip, 109
Stephens, Suzanne, 43
Stetzel, Warren, 137
Strip mining, 19, 99
Suburbs, 36

Takama, Saburo, 132
Termites, 117–118
Thermal mass of concrete, 144
Thoreau, Henry, 2–3

Three Mile Island (Pa.), 9, 93
Toilets, 29, 32
Topsoil, 159
Total Environmental Action (TEA), 133
Tree removal, 160
Trees, 100–102

Underground architecture, 61, 69–80
Underground highways, 91–92
Underground office buildings, 17, 23, 25–27
Underground Space (AUSA), 61
Urban mining, 87–88

Values:
  responsible living based on, 6–9
  (*See also* Wilderness Values)
Venturi, Robert, 29
Vinyl, 53

Waste management, 39, 87–88, 154–155
Water:
  carcinogens in, 97–98
  management of, 38, 56–57, 159–160
  quality standards, 96

Water *(Cont.)*:
  waste of, 68–69
Waterless toilets, 32
Watson, Donald, 71, 109, 165
Wells, Kappy, 51
Whitman, Walt, 100
Wilderness values, 28–30, 33–40, 54
  checklist for, 38–40
  evaluation of, 34–37
Wildlife, protection of, 40, 159
Wind power, 29
Windows, 155–156
  insulation of, 120–122
  small, 119–120
Winter of 1976–1977, 109
Wood, 148–150
Wood preservatives, 157
Wood stoves, 150
World's Fair (N.Y.) (1964), 22, 85
Wright, Frank Lloyd, 28, 44, 47, 63, 120

Yanda, Bill, 86

Zoning:
  discriminatory, 56
  nondegradation standards for, 54